Is College a Lousy Investment?

Is College a Lousy Investment?

Negotiating the Hidden Costs of Higher Education

Tara Jabbaar-Gyambrah and Seneca Vaught

ROWMAN & LITTLEFIELD
Lanham • Boulder • New York • London

Published by Rowman & Littlefield
A wholly owned subsidiary of The Rowman & Littlefield Publishing Group, Inc.
4501 Forbes Boulevard, Suite 200, Lanham, Maryland 20706
www.rowman.com

Unit A, Whitacre Mews, 26-34 Stannary Street, London SE11 4AB

Copyright © 2018 by Tara Jabbaar-Gyambrah and Seneca Vaught

All rights reserved. No part of this book may be reproduced in any form or by any electronic or mechanical means, including information storage and retrieval systems, without written permission from the publisher, except by a reviewer who may quote passages in a review.

British Library Cataloguing in Publication Information Available

Library of Congress Cataloging-in-Publication Data Is Available

ISBN 978-1-4758-3397-3 (cloth: alk. paper)
ISBN 978-1-4758-3398-0 (pbk: alk. paper)
ISBN 978-1-4758-3399-7 (electronic)

∞ ™ The paper used in this publication meets the minimum requirements of American National Standard for Information Sciences Permanence of Paper for Printed Library Materials, ANSI/NISO Z39.48-1992.

Printed in the United States of America

This book is dedicated to all the families, students, counselors, and others who strive to make an investment in their future.

Contents

Preface	ix
Acknowledgments	xiii
Introduction	xv
1 Why Does College Cost So Much? : The High Price of Higher Learning	1
2 What Happens When You Major for Money?: The Guild Mindset versus an (Inter)Disciplinary Mentality	15
3 Why Are American Universities So Expensive?: Getting What You Pay For	33
4 Who Pays the Most for College?: At the Heart of Inequality	43
5 What Is Your College Education Worth?: The Dangers of Investment Mentalities and Jargon on Higher Learning	53
6 Why Is It Important to Invest in Yourself?: Success Strategies for When the College Bubble Bursts	67
Conclusion	79
Bibliography	83
About the Authors	91

Preface

Together we have over twenty-five years of experience in higher education at private, public, nonprofit, and for-profit institutions. Based on a series of ongoing conversations and trends in higher education, we decided to write *Is College a Lousy Investment?: Negotiating the Hidden Costs of Higher Education* to share what we have encountered personally and professionally as it relates to college life. One of the key concerns raised by employers, parents, and educators consistently centers on the notion of college as an investment. In this book, we want to provide a practitioner's context for analyzing this idea and its impact.

Within the last ten years there has been an explosion in the number of books written about the purpose of a college education and its affordability. *Academically Adrift, Breaking Point: The College Affordability Crisis and Our Next Financial Bubble*, and *Stretching the Higher Ed Dollar* have all addressed rising anxieties about the value of college. The works that have been most popular address questions about the escalating cost of college and whether a degree is still a wise choice. The underlying questions they all pose are is a college degree worth it, and what is the true value of a college degree?

In this book, we ask two equally important questions. How can students, parents, and counselors think about higher education as an investment to make the kind of decisions that treat college as a major financial decision? If college is the most important economic decision many people will make during their lifetime, what can be done to maximize the return on the investment and to better align it with personal goals and economic expectations?

We have six major answers to these questions that we address in each chapter of this book. The book serves as a roadmap to guide parents and advisors to the solutions that will help students maximize their time and money in higher education:

- We examine what parents, advisors, and students mean when they talk about the worth of a college degree. We give parents a set of guided questions for their students before they spend a dime on their college education.
- The solutions we pose require a rethinking of the college diploma as something more than a receipt or a ticket to a job. We give a matrix of how to align aptitude and interest with career aspirations.
- We discuss how parents and students can get the most from tuition dollars. We provide a holistic formula to determine if students are getting what they assume they are paying for.
- The solutions we pose help students avoid the pitfalls of high debt and living in their parents' basement after college. We give a college blueprint plan on how to pay for college while learning to negotiate like an entrepreneur.
- We discuss how parents and students should evaluate various aspects of the college experience if they expect higher education to pay off. We provide a list of high-impact practices that add to the so-called return on investment when incorporated into the educational portfolio.
- We provide the rationale for problem-oriented and lifelong learning instead of a dropout mentality. We provide a series of case studies that help students compete in a global marketplace where passion and purposeful experiences are increasingly more important than degrees.

Americans have increasingly thought of college as an investment because of its spiraling costs. The College Board releases the trends in pricing on colleges for both public and private institutions yearly. For the 2016-2017 academic year, the cost for a college education from a public four-year in-state school was about $20,090 including tuition, room and board, plus fees. A private four-year in-state college education costs much more, averaging $45,370 for a four-year degree.[1]

The costs of both private and public institutions have increased dramatically over the last ten years by over $10,000. In 2006, the average cost of a public four-year in-state college degree was about $12,796, while four-year private in-state was $30,367.[2] Private institutions increased the most, by over $14,000. We are questioning the worth of what our students are getting, as young adults who are often too young to consume alcoholic beverages are now being asked to sign away decades' worth of their future earnings.

The decision to attend college comes with a great level of risk that is often ignored in favor of certain assumptions about economic benefits. College graduates make hundreds of thousands of dollars more over their lifetime than those without a degree. However, the increasing difficulty that many graduates experience in finding high-paying jobs has become a major challenge. Some ask, Why bother? Is it worth it?

In each chapter we will use pseudonyms of typical students we have encountered. These case studies provide data-based examples of students making decisions about college. For example, James and Sonya represent two typical students. Both of these students have goals of career success based on a deep-seated belief that college is an investment. James is returning to college after working in construction for the past three years. He has aspirations of becoming a pharmacist. Sonya just graduated at the top of her class in the spring and wants to join the incoming class of aspiring engineers at Somewhere University in the fall.

Both James and Sonya view a college degree as their ticket to an increased income and standard of living, but their experiences and expectations will heavily factor into whether they will realize their goals. Most people believe that most college students begin within a year of graduating from high school, like Sonya—in reality, only around 5 percent do and live on campus. The typical college student is much more like James, having worked or taken a break before pursuing higher education.[3]

There is nothing wrong with viewing college as a way to improve one's standard of living. However, the increasing tendency for students, parents, and educators to interpret the sole role of college as a guarantor of upward mobility may have introduced a whole range of assumptions that undermine the historical role of colleges and universities and what they are able to deliver given their current configurations.

These students presented in the example are typical of most students attending college today. In the early 2000s there was an explosion in the number of books written about the purpose of a college education and its affordability. Additionally, a growing body of work—such as *College (UN)Bound*; *Fall of the Faculty*; *College: What It Was, Is, and Should Be*; *American Higher Education Crisis*; and *The End of College*—suggested that college itself was undergoing a crisis. Works in this body of literature have engaged questions about the broader role of a college education, escalating cost, and accessibility for the American public. The ultimate question emerges: Is college worth it?

Since the 1970s, Americans have tended to approach college with a fiscally oriented mind-set, which has fundamentally changed the historical function of higher education for the worse. Viewing college solely as a way of increasing one's earnings was not entirely new, but the increasing emphasis on training came at the expense of other historical missions of the university.

PayScale's ranking of colleges and universities based on similar economic indicators gained the attention of the White House as a possible tool for evaluating the disbursement of financial aid. This shift signaled a shift in the national dialogue on higher education, in which the transformative aspects of college have been replaced with a one-dimensional obsession with salary and credentialization.[4]

Our hope is to provide additional context to this new chapter of college history as an investment from a different perspective. We hope this book serves as a holistic resource for parents and counselors who are closely involved with the decision making of students as it relates to their career choices and the most important economic decision students will make in their lives.

NOTES

1. "Trends in College Pricing 2016," accessed December 29, 2016, https://trends.collegeboard.org/sites/default/files/2016-trends-college-pricing-web_0.pdf.

2. "Trends in College Pricing 2006," accessed December 29, 2016, http://trends.collegeboard.org/sites/default/files/CP_2006.pdf.

3. Conor Friedersdorf, "The Typical College Student Is Not Who You Think It Is," *The Atlantic*, July 1, 2016, https://www.theatlantic.com/education/archive/2016/07/the-typical-college-student-is-not-who-you-think-it-is/489824/.

4. Jack Stripling, "Obama's Legacy: An Unlikely Hawk on Higher Ed," *The Chronicle of Higher Education*, September 25, 2016; Anthony P. Carnevale, Jeff Strohl, Michelle Melton, and Center on Education and the Workforce Georgetown University, "Selected Findings from What's It Worth? The Economic Value of College Majors," Georgetown University Center on Education and the Workforce, January 1, 2011. Georgetown University Center on Education and the Workforce, 3300 Whitehaven Street NW, Suite 5000 Box 571444, Washington, DC 20057. Tel: 202-687-4922; Fax: 202-687-3110; email: cewgeorgetown@georgetown.edu; website: http://cew.georgetown.edu ; Courtney Connley, "Is Your Degree Worth the Investment?" *Black Enterprise* 46, no. 2 (September 2015): 52–54; Barbara Fenesi and Faria Sana, "What Is Your Degree Worth? The Relationship between Post-Secondary Programs and Employment Outcomes," *Canadian Journal of Higher Education* 45, no. 4 (January 1, 2015): 383–99; Robert J. Thornton, "What's Your College Degree Worth? A Research Project for the Labor Economics Course," *Journal of Economic Education* 40, no. 2 (Spring 2009): 166–72.

Acknowledgments

We are extremely grateful to our many supporters of our book project who helped it to come to life. First and foremost, we thank God and the Lord Jesus Christ our Savior for the opportunity to write this book. Also, we thank the Rowman & Littlefield family; the National Association for College Admission Counseling (NACAC) for believing in our project in its earliest form; the Center for Excellence in Teaching and Learning and the First Year and Transitions Program at Kennesaw State University; our reviewers Kendra Cadogan, Dr. Jeannine Dingus-Eason, Dr. Christopher Holoman, Bridget Hodges, Dr. Mwalimu J. Shujaa, and Tommy McClam; and our family and friends. We would not have been able to complete this project without your support.

Introduction

WHAT THIS BOOK IS ABOUT

Our goal in this book is to shift the discussion about the role of college away from shallow and unexamined economic assumptions. We want to expose how these financial misconceptions impact the reality of millions of students. This book delves into the controversy surrounding how students should best capitalize on the value of a college degree and select majors based on a variety of evidence and interdisciplinary interpretations of data.

Each chapter discusses the experiences of typical students who represent significant proportions of higher education demographics. We extrapolate personal stories that narrate the data analyzing the modern crisis in higher education. While the specific stories are fictional, these profiles are developed from data in the literature and firsthand composite accounts of students, parents, professors, and educational professionals we have encountered.

Numerous proponents of the so-called human-capital theory have sought to theorize the benefits and value of higher education. This is not our approach. As this text outlines, we remain very critical of attempts to quantify the worth of college in purely transactional terms. In other words, we argue that college is much more valuable than what it pretends to sell. This book outlines caveat emptor, a warning for buyers of college diplomas to beware.

Like the Latin phrase above, we see an overabundance of economic jargon being used to describe the college experience. Often these terms are deceptive and mislead students, parents, and policymakers to have unrealistic expectations. This book challenges the assumptions implied in common catchphrases people use to discuss college (e.g., the worth of a college degree, good return on your college investment) to probe the underlying questions students have.

The central question of this book runs counter to popular views about college as an investment. We argue that investment approaches have often neglected the true value of a college education and sidelined the most formative aspects of a college experience. Consequently, many who hold such views leave college less educated and also less economically empowered to achieve the monetary goals that attracted them to college in the first place. Our book explores why this is the case and what to do about it.

SITUATING THE ARGUMENT

Jeffrey J. Selingo's *College (Un)Bound* (2013) argues that higher educational institutions in the United States were not navigating challenges of the 2008 fiscal crisis particularly well due to habits established long before the economic collapse. For Selingo, colleges have been driven by the wrong factors, causing increased costs for students and failure to deliver a solid return on investment. The factors were further explored in Andrew Rossi's award-winning documentary *Ivory Tower* (2014).

Unlike Rossi, Selingo hints that the future of college will largely be outsourced piecemeal into the hands of massive open online courses (MOOCs), no-frills degree mills, and other online alternatives. Within each of these innovative approaches, there is an emphasis on practical experiences, the student transition to college, increased access to the local community, and engagement of the "big questions" that relate to student goals and career objectives.

While Selingo is optimistic about the opportunity to address many of these problems through scaled-back, technologically savvy models, his approach raises important questions that must be addressed in the meantime. What are ways that colleges/universities can ensure that all students are obtaining their return on investment now? How can students make the most of their college experiences today?

FROM A RETURN ON INVESTMENT TO AN UNCERTAIN FUTURE

There is an abundance of auxiliary services that help students analyze how to afford the rising cost of college. *Forbes* offers a tool that helps calculate the cost of a degree. PayScale provides an important list for evaluating the return on investment (ROI) in a national ranking system that has received much attention. Bankrate estimates the value of the college degree by numerical breakdown of its costs, time it takes to repay the investment, and years expected to complete the college degree.[1] However, all of these economic tools ignore an essential factor.

The most enduring value of a college education is the diverse network of friends and acquaintances—personal and professional—that one makes and will continue to draw on for the indefinite future. Already, many underrepresented groups find themselves at a disadvantage because they lack these connections when they get to college and are challenged to find sustaining mentors while enrolled. College at the core provides opportunities for creative connectivity and serendipitous spontaneity.

For many, the social experience of college is the last barrier between adolescence and adulthood. The interactions that occur between professors and between students on a personal level are valuable beyond the content of the course or the exchange of money for a grade. In an age when social skills are arguably in decline amidst a generation that would rather text than talk, or troll than publicly debate, these concerns raise serious questions about the future not only of the workplace but of a functional democracy.

Former Education Secretary William Bennett (2013) makes a convincing case against universal college education in *Is College Worth It?* At the core of Bennett's arguments are three assertions: first, that viewed from the perspective of an investment, most students are unemployed upon graduation and do not receive immediate returns on the money spent on college; second, that college is not for everyone but depends on a variety of factors that include a student's educational ability and finances; finally, that the limited learning taking place on college campuses does not justify the high cost.

What is problematic with Bennett's approach is that it also deceptively relies on an approach to college as a transactional financial instrument. In a market-driven society, it is useful to think about one of the largest investments in one's life in these terms, but thinking about college in this manner becomes problematic when one proceeds to the logical conclusion. College does not pay to whom we expect, in the ways we expect, and when we expect it—and it never has.

In many ways, Bennett's market-driven conclusion was prophesied by David Labaree in 1997. Labaree worried that thinking about colleges as a private investment rather than a public one would displace many of the fundamental attitudes necessary for both personal transformation and the public good. The professional goals that prompt students to invest in a college education are not wrong in themselves but become problematic when those personal ambitions trump everything else.[2]

In his words, "The biggest threat facing American schools is not the conflict, contradiction, and compromise that arise from trying to keep a balance among educational goals." Instead, he argues, "the main threat comes from the growing dominance of the social mobility goal over the others.... The increasing hegemony of the mobility goal and its narrow consumer-based approach to education have led to the re-conceptualization of education as a purely private good."[3]

Larabee's conclusion relates directly to current concerns about the college crisis. The investment mentality has transmogrified college into a personal financial vending machine. Students are making bad decisions about the colleges (fund managers), degrees (portfolios), and courses (equities) to be traded. This mental framework reveals much about changing perceptions of education and undermines the very existence of education.

ORGANIZATION OF THE BOOK

This book is divided into six chapters that address this fundamental problem. Chapter 1 examines the underestimated costs and hidden value of the college experience. We examine the social role of college and the importance of academic expertise in guiding novices through a deluge of knowledge. We discuss how unrealistic expectations about the role of college as an investment are reflected in societal perceptions of higher education and student behavior.

Chapter 2 discusses how the widely accepted approach to college as an investment tends to emphasize technical mastery over meta-thinking and self-directed learning. This view raises some key concerns about how investment advocates think of college as receivership rather than a quest for disciplinary mastery and intellectual development.

In chapter 3, we examine popular arguments that students are "not receiving what they have paid for" as a paradoxical assumption. We contend that students are receiving exactly what they are paying for, which is often superficial (e.g., football, dorms, rock climbing walls, etc.). This results in more student loan debt, higher unemployment rates, and a so-called lack of real-life skills that could help students develop their career portfolio.

Chapter 4 delves into why economic discussions about student loan-to-debt ratios and the "worthless liberal arts degree" can be misleading. We also explore the unequal burden of financing a college education in underrepresented communities and what this challenge tells us about the true value of education.

Chapter 5 discusses the ways in which students view college as a "ticket" item for financial success. Unfortunately, college cannot be articulated into a solid return on investment unless students understand the true value of their educational experiences and invest in meaningful interactions.

Chapter 6 examines shortcomings of data-based arguments that college is no longer a sound financial investment on economic grounds. If we were to apply the same logic to financial investments, the inconsistencies become more apparent of what we may realistically expect economic returns from a college degree to supply.

Our final chapter hones in on educational and financial strategies to negotiate the rising costs of higher education. We illustrate how successful certain types of students have been in building a strong academic, professional, and personal portfolio without the accumulation of debt. The stories in this chapter illustrate that students can use all of their experiences to maximize their potential both financially and intellectually by using more holistic measurements of success.

NOTES

1. Chris Kahn, "What Is the ROI of Your College Degree," *Money Pulse*, accessed January 1, 2017, http://www.bankrate.com/finance/college-finance/roi-college-degree.aspx.
2. David F. Labaree, *How to Succeed in School Without Really Learning: The Credentials Race in American Education* (New Haven, CT: Yale University Press, 1997).
3. Ibid., 73.

Chapter One

Why Does College Cost So Much?

The High Price of Higher Learning

Jason is the first in his family of four to attend college. He is white, eighteen years old, and from Ohio. Both of Jason's parents work full-time but their combined income is less than $75,000 per year. Like many students in this demographic, his exposure to college arose when a family member started college but was unable to stay enrolled. Jason has high expectations that college will transport him to the middle-class lifestyle of his dreams and sees getting a degree quickly as a priority. However, he knows very little about the cost of college.[1]

Jason thinks he is well prepared to attend college. He has decent grades and above average test scores, and he has followed the recommendations of his advisors and counselors. Our first-generation student is well prepared academically but has not asked how college will help him meet his economic expectations. He assumes that just getting accepted into any college will be worth it.

Jason is overjoyed when he receives a letter of acceptance to Somewhere University but has no idea that the next leg of his educational journey will require him to finance 80 percent of his living expenses. In two years, he will have relied on help from his parents to finance part of his education with private loans. Unbeknownst to Jason, his decision to attend Somewhere University will cost him about 30 percent of his future earnings per month over the next thirty years after he graduates. In other words, nearly one-third of his salary for the next three decades will be dedicated to servicing student loan debt. This will directly impact his ability to own a home, buy a car, and start a family.[2]

Jason does not think about his college experience as an uncertain financial investment. His four-year commitment to go to college is comparable to the experiences of indentured servants who came to the American colonies seeking a better life, generations ago. Similar to the terms of an indenture, Jason has pledged to working on a degree for a fixed period of time for an economic reward at the end. He has hopes that his hard work will lead to a fulfilling career.

Jason's decision to embark on a new station in life is based on his ideas about the worth of education. He sees college as an apprenticeship and an education in exchange for future freedom and economic reward. Indentured servants agreed to terms that essentially signed away a period of their life by agreeing to work for several years.[3] Their contracts sacrificed their present for hopes of economic prosperity in the future.

Where Jason's historical predecessors' situation was different than Jason's is that their debt was erased at the end of their term of indenture. Jason will face a large amount of student loan debt that will diminish his hopes of a more prosperous life. As Jason contemplates the cost of education at Somewhere University, he makes assumptions that despite the investment of time and money, once completing his degree he will get a job. It is somewhat of a gamble but the risk is one worth taking because of the potential opportunities on the other side of the degree.

Jason's story examines the underestimated hidden costs of a college education. This chapter explores what parents, advisors, and students mean when they talk about the cost, worth, and value of a college degree. Also incorporated in this chapter is a set of guided questions for parents to discuss with their student. These are financially important items that parents should consider before they spend a dime on their student's college education.

Jason's journey is similar to one faced by thousands of families across the country. Every year, millions of students not yet old enough to legally consume alcoholic beverages sign promissory notes that will be one of the *most important monetary commitments* of their financial lives. This is a disturbing fact with serious consequences regarding the worth of a college degree.

Numerous scholars such as Sara Goldrick-Rab, Robert B. Archbald, and Robert Samuels have increasingly pointed to the major economic responsibility that thousands of students consign themselves to.[4] The students make serious financial decisions without having the adequate information or foresight to understand how these choices will continue to impact them for the next thirty years. How students choose to finance their education will impact the types of jobs that they will get; the amount of income they will earn; where they will live; who, when, and if they will marry; and even whether they will decide to grow a family.

PRICING THE WORTH AND COST OF COLLEGE

Since the 1990s, students have increasingly borne the rising costs of higher education in the form of student loans. For example, in 1992–1993, the average student debt obligation was $12,434.[5] By 2016, that load had increased to $30,100,[6] nearly tripling the amount of student loans nationally. Parents have also increasingly helped their children finance the cost of a college education with private loans. The Parent Plus loan, for example, has become a very popular way to finance college education; in 2014 over $10 million was borrowed to finance students' education.[7]

In arrangements eerily reminiscent of sharecropping and the crop-lien system, some students are turning to income-sharing agreements in which they agree to pay a fixed portion of their income to investors who cover their tuition and education costs.[8] Private investment companies are developing financial instruments that offer to finance a student's degree in exchange for a defined percentage of future income. This arrangement is the opposite of indentured servitude. It proposes a plan of indefinite debt while providing no relief for students.

Critics have suggested that the price of higher education is grossly inflated and that students would be better off skipping college altogether. One study, "Is College Worth It," revealed that 75 percent of Americans cannot afford college education and it does not provide good value for the money spent.[9] Another study through Goldman suggested college is not worth it because of the exorbitant costs and students that go to the bottom 25 percent of colleges do not earn as much as their counterparts.[10]

However, despite this evidence many parents and students continue to feel that college is worth paying any cost, even amidst increases in post-college unemployment rates, migration of job opportunities to urban areas and overseas, and high-cost rental markets, among other issues. But what do these costs and the willingness of a steady supply of students to pay it reveal about its value? Many students are aware of these factors but still feel that college is worth the cost because they are desperate for ideas to improve their financial situation.

The sheer sum of money required to attend college in recent years has prompted Jason and many students like him to ask, Why does college cost so much? What are *other costs* of higher education worth considering? Instead of framing these costs in the usual financial terms, we need to also account for the hidden cost that students, parents, and educators pay for the current educational environment. The hidden costs of student loans have prevented students from achieving the American dream and reaching their academic potential.

College is very expensive, but one reason that people are willing to pay for it is they believe that there are benefits worth the cost. They know that the price of forgoing a college education will have severe economic impacts that limit job opportunities. While it is true that not all students should go to college, the decision to attend college should be well considered in the context of a variety of economic factors.[11]

One reason for this is that the true worth of educational experiences is significantly undervalued by Americans in relation to what college credentials signify. As most colleges have adopted consumer-based models, parents and students look to higher education to guarantee access to high-paying jobs after students complete their degrees. Ironically, there is little concern for the learning experience (e.g., critical thinking skills, cultural sophistication, lifelong learning mentality, problem solving skills) that makes college students in high demand.

Since the emergence of consumer-based models of education in the 1980s, colleges have marketed the commercial aspects of delivering a certain lifestyle to their customers.[12] In turn, students and parents have changed the emphasis from aspects of *learning* to the benefits of *earning* of a degree. Inevitably, students have become passive cogs in corporatized institutions once designed to train minds to create and repair the social machinery of democracy.

Higher education has played into this consumer model of education by undermining the social benefits of disciplines and the historical missions of the university. Many institutions have substituted slick marketing and satisfaction surveys above the hard and elusive truths of a well-rounded college education. For example, colleges often market the idea of finishing a college degree within four years as a guarantee. Does this gimmick actually guarantee anything of value? Perhaps some students are better off taking more time to complete a degree.

Thinking of college as a personal return on investment and promoting it this way severely undermines the potential of both individuals and the institution. If parents, students, and policymakers desire a broad educational base for sustainable economic growth, it will require a much closer accounting of the value of college beyond the possibilities of today's job market. Students and colleges must be accountable to each other in ways not yet imagined.

COST ACCOUNTABILITY IN COLLEGES AND UNIVERSITIES

High college tuition rates are vilified but there is little understanding of what has led to these costs and how monies have been spent. Colleges and universities must be accountable for how they spend tuition dollars. The vast complexity of fiscal policies in public and private colleges (not to mention for-profit institutions) is not easy to access, let alone comprehend. Most parents and students don't understand how a combination of federal, state, and tuition dollars fund their institutions and what that means as a collective investment in the public good.

Parents and students seldom focus on questions that expose the true cost of a university's priorities, such as: faculty-to-student ratios, the ratio of full-time teaching faculty to part-time faculty, graduation rates, academic advising support, and student support services. Higher educational institutions rarely present this information upfront. Students and parents should not be distracted when colleges center on the profitability of majors offered, scholarship money, and the sticker price without addressing these priorities.

In addition to financial costs, attendance at American institutions often requires students to sacrifice much more than cash and future earnings. Joining the ranks of the college bound increasingly requires students to deny their intellectual passions and substitute these aspirations for what is financially feasible at the moment. Students need not completely disregard the financial aspects of a particular field of study, but to completely ignore the time-tested benefits of a broad liberal arts curriculum in substitution for fads in the marketplace is a costly tragedy.

With the growth of business colleges, nursing programs, and engineering specialties, the expectation of college has become more focused on specialized training. All of these fields have their place, but the true value of college remains in the opportunities they provide for broad-based intellectual exploration and personal transformation. Scarce resources in higher education are often wasted on what could be more efficiently completed in job-site training programs. Is it wise for students to embark on a four-year degree at a higher cost for the hyper-specialized kinds of training that can be completed on the job in weeks or months?

Consequently, many students and parents feel that they can no longer afford to explore or be intellectually curious. Who can blame them? In the current crisis, rising tuition costs make the intellectual wandering that has characterized modern college life for decades seem financially irresponsible. Why would anyone pay so much for the intangible benefits of learning when there are loans to repay tomorrow? Time is money. Only certain majors can promise a return on investment today.

Americans have such individualized notions of their relationship to college, they do not understand the broader connections between the cost of public investments in the private good. There is deep worth in the diverse communal aspects of college life that are significantly undervalued in the assessment of price and other economic indicators. College students live together, eat together, study together, and play together in a high-stress and high-stakes environment. Students learn to relate and to work out their problems in cooperation with others.

Students who attend college are much better off socially because they will come into close contact with a variety of other people with different beliefs, backgrounds, and ideas.[13] For many students this is the first time that they encounter people different from themselves. This experience is invaluable because it helps them develop intercultural and interpersonal skills that will help them relate to diverse populations they will encounter in the global marketplace.

This type of experience is a significant part of why college is so valuable. College is the place where students begin to understand the perspectives of others in relation to the world that challenges them to develop new ideas. The intercultural shuffling effect of college can have an important impact on the social evolution of young people in ways that are not easily measured in economic terms. While there is certainly worth in students being able to understand and to relate to a variety of people who are different from themselves, the cost of not having this experience is probably easier to assess.

There are diverse communities across the United States that have very low ratios of college students in relation to the broader population. These communities are in peril economically and have been in peril for some time. The census data reveals that the economic indicators of communities with very low numbers of college graduates are much lower than those who have college education.[14] While it would be misleading to suggest that a college education alone is sufficient to transform a community's economic prospects, communities that lack college graduates suffer economically but also culturally.

THE COST OF CULTURE

The notion of diversity as an extracurricular offering undervalues the true worth of a college education. Too many parents and students fail to incorporate the value of a range of social skills that students develop while in college into their assessment of what college is worth. It is widely perceived that students go to college to grow up, but what does that mean? What are the economic costs of this social maturity?

College experiences expose students to a variety of perspectives and teach them to adjust to rapid changes in the economy and in work. The collective social, cultural, and economic benefits that can be derived from college are very difficult to attain elsewhere. As we will explore in a later chapter, those who have managed to navigate much of their lives without a college education often return to explore courses that undergird the collective culture.

It is very common to see nontraditional students, as we call them, enrolling in various courses in history, arts, and the humanities. The National Center for Education Statistics defines nontraditional students as pupils working part-time or having delayed their entrance to college but also includes many other factors.[15] Contrary to popular belief, nearly half of the students enrolled in higher education today are nontraditional. These students have often come to terms with a more complete understanding of the role of college but are often very focused on economic value.

This community of nontraditional students includes people like Jason. However, this also includes adult students who are older than him who have been to college and dropped out only to return later in life. Both groups found that the social and economic costs for not investing in college are too high. These demographics often bring an investment mind-set to college than can prevent students from fully seizing the benefits that college brings. In the last decade, students have tended to focus exclusively on shortsighted economic goals at the expense of longer-term interrelated social and developmental goals.

While this may seem to be counterintuitive to readers who attended college in the last century, most twenty-first-century college students have this mind-set. Students choose majors solely based on expected jobs. As a result, they narrow their focus to avoid other experiences that offer a more holistic approach to learning. In doing so, students are so focused on personal ambitions to make money that they may be preventing themselves from engaging the types of deep learning experiences that will be the most profitable in the long run.

THE VALUE OF A NEW COLLEGE MIND-SET

What if there was a different mind-set about the purpose of obtaining an education? The current goal for many students in college today is not to be transformed. Instead, they want validation of what they already know. These sentiments are not unique but are certainly characteristic of a certain type of student in college, like Jason, who views the true cost of learning as an affirmation of his abilities.

Jason's mind-set comes with certain psychological costs as students approach college. American students often assume that they know much more than they actually do in comparison to their international peers. Repeatedly, American students have ranked themselves very high in their self-assessment of knowledge even when that does not bear out in comparison to their international peers.[16] Consequently, every year many students approach college with the mind-set that there is little that they can learn other than how to endure the ordeal.

Americans must become part of a broader international dialogue to understand the competitiveness of college but also to develop the types of multicultural, multidisciplinary, and multinational coalitions that the future of the world depends upon. To do so will require people to shift the understanding of college from that of a personal vending machine to an interconnected academic hub. This is a paradigm shift that will require a reevaluation of the role of information and the investment mind-set.

In his book *Is College Worth It?*, Bennett says that students are not making good decisions about college as it relates to cost and curriculum selection.[17] At the same time, they have more information available than at any prior point in history. Bennett argues that students have the ability to go to a library or the Internet to get the equivalent of a college education. Herein lies the problem. Bennett and others who argue that knowledge is readily available and conclude that college is overpriced or unnecessary underestimate the hidden cost of expertise and its invisible role in guiding novices through a deluge of knowledge.

In other words, those who argue that college is a bad investment and say that students can readily access free information often fail to acknowledge the reason why students do not have access: they do not know how or they cannot find out how to get access. Investing in college is about learning to collect information but also about learning to live and relate with others in a diverse knowledge economy. College is a place where students learn how to transform knowledge in various ways and how to process it with others.

If we were to take a deeper look at what Bennett is saying about knowledge, there is a bit of truth in it. There is in fact an overabundance of information ready to be absorbed and put into action, but self-directed education doesn't yield the same results as a college education. While higher education institutions provide foundational knowledge on how to succeed in society's workforce, many colleges fail to incentivize the "how to" and practical experiences that encourage lifelong learning after students have finished their education.

This is why there are so many students like Jason taking a gap year either right after high school or right after college. These students are not yet sure about who they are, what skills they possess, and how they should proceed with their careers. Parents and advisors must be mindful of these challenges as they support students considering their options. Today's college students face decisions about the financial and opportunity costs of college that were unconsidered in the past.

In *There Is Life After College* (2016), Jeffrey Selingo posits that students have lived a structured life where everything has been planned for them before and during college life. As a result, students often lack time management skills and the ability to work independently on projects and end up not really knowing what they want to do in life. He also mentions that college students have not taken advantage of the wealth of knowledge and expertise of faculty and staff at higher education institutions. In his words, they [college students] fail to cultivate relationships with professors or staff on campus who might lend advice and act as mentors. And they are reluctant to chase after experiences—whether undergraduate research, study abroad, or internships—that help them discover their passions and arm them with the interpersonal skills so in demand by employers today.[18]

So, what if high schools and college students did not have a structured schedule but built their own experiences in college based on the areas of study they want to pursue, their passions, and core strengths? What if there was an opportunity for students to spend time exploring and figuring out who they are before deciding what major is right for them? And what if students understood the true value of cultivating relationships with faculty and staff as mentors that would provide them with mentorship?

This burden is not the sole responsibility of students. This was the major lapse in Gene Marks's 2011 *Forbes* essay, "If I Were a Poor Black Kid." Marks, who supports the importance of a college education for underrepresented students, missed what so many education reductionists also fail to consider. By minimizing education to a transaction, a checklist of mere activities and credentials, the environment of expertise and inquiry, often assumed to be universal by society's most privileged, becomes invisible.

Education, especially for the most underserved communities, is more than content, it is also context. Learning is not just an issue of having access to content, or technology for that matter, but having the critical environment and intellectual support so that the subject becomes self-aware and interconnected.

THE PRICE OF AN INVESTMENT MIND-SET

As more Americans have approached a college education with a purely fiscal-oriented mind-set, that expectation has fundamentally changed the character of higher education for the worse. One reason for this is that people see little social value in college. As a result, the overarching premise for a college education has drastically shifted in the last fifty years from one that emphasizes acculturation and civic values to one that puts an emphasis on career advancement and economic empowerment.

Viewing college as a way of increasing one's earnings is not entirely new, but the increasing emphasis on training has arrived at the expense of other historical missions of the university that paradoxically had broader cost for the rest of society. The federal government has increased funding for public education steadily over the last fifty years under both Republican and Democratic administrations. However, these "investments" have not satisfied taxpayers because the expectation of education is largely different. Consequently, the return-on-investment mentality is based on unrealistic expectations that Americans as consumers have about a college education.

Facing the sticker price of rising college tuitions, Americans expect a return on the dollars invested in college with much less patience than they have with their funds in a 401(k), equities, or bonds. Few Americans would expect to get a 100 percent return on these types of investments yet they regularly expect that college degrees will pay off immediately after the money is spent. These expectations have increasingly led to draconian policies, administrative practices, and estimations of the value of certain programs and degrees in rather misleading analogies.

Even so, the time that it takes to recoup dollars from college education has been steadily declining from the 1970s. Several studies have shown that students, after seeing no immediate economic benefits during the four to six years of full-time enrollment, begin to realize economic benefits in salary in as little as four years after graduation.[19] This expectation is unrealistic but understandable given the high cost of college and the immediacy of repaying student loans after graduation.

CONCLUSION

Every year hundreds of thousands of Americans applaud their sons and their daughters at commencement exercises across the country. These ceremonies are the capstone of achievement and ring with a certain sense of accomplishment. However, behind the pomp and circumstance, we find an American society deeply at odds with the price and promise of education.

It has often been said that colleges are training students today for the jobs of tomorrow that do not yet exist. Colleges that are in tune with this goal must be more flexible and more closely associated with their unique role in the international marketplace of ideas. Likewise, students who will succeed in tomorrow's economy must take the lead in expanding our narrow-minded assumptions about the role of college today.

Parent and Advisor Smart Investment Guided Questions

In order to assist students with preparing for their investment in college, the following guided questions challenge students to think critically about their own personal and professional growth while providing practical advice that is immediately applicable. Take a few days and ask your student to answer the questions in the guide.

- How are you developing interpersonal skills? In what ways do you think social skills can help you navigate your career pathway? What is the

importance of developing intercultural competency communication in today's ever changing society?
- Are you willing to sacrifice a third of your salary to pay for student loan debt?
- Are you willing to give up four years of your life? What are you going to miss out on during that time period? What might you gain that will make it worthwhile?
- What are your expectations for life after college? How much would it cost you in very specific terms (e.g., mortgage, car note, etc.)? And how will college help you achieve this lifestyle? How will the cost of college or repaying student loans impact this plan?
- If you had $30,000 to spend on anything, what would it be? How can you approach college with this type of mind-set? How can you best spend this money in learning experiences in ways that will pay you back?
- What is the value that you place on non-career-specific skills such as critical thinking, literacy, and problem solving? How are people whom you aspire to be like more than the product of a narrow field of study or a particular degree?
- What do you know about how your tuition dollars are spent at the college you would like to attend or currently are enrolled in? What are the faculty-to-student ratios, the ratio of full-time teaching faculty to part-time faculty, graduation rates, academic advising, and student support services? Is your college choice investing as much in your learning experiences as you are?
- How much has your college invested in providing a diverse learning environment with people of different backgrounds? How do they provide opportunities to develop diverse interpersonal networks? Are there opportunities for deep life-altering experiences rather than just the rote transfer of knowledge? What type of opportunities for mentoring and community learning does this institution invest in?

Action Steps

Investing in college is a very important decision for every student. It requires time, commitment, and research to select the right college/university that aligns with the student's interest, passion, and career goals.

1. Students should closely evaluate their passion and interests while in high school. Taking time to discover who they really are early on will be helpful when applying to college.
2. Students should get involved in activities that may or may not interest them. This will help them learn about their likes and dislikes.

3. Students should set S.M.A.R.T. (Specific, Measurable, Achievable, Results-focused, and Time-bound) goals each year based on their personal and professional life.
4. Students should work with a coach, their parents, and school counselor to develop a plan for their future.

NOTES

1. Ernest T. Pascarella et al., "First-Generation College Students: Additional Evidence on College Experiences and Outcomes," *The Journal of Higher Education* 75, no. 3 (2004): 250-51; Ashley Smith, "Who's in First (Generation)?," *Insider HigherEd*, November 10, 2015, accessed March 16, 2017, https://www.insidehighered.com/news/2015/11/10/who-are-first-generation-students-and-how-do-they-fare.

2. Alvaro Mezza, Daniel R. Ringo, Shane M. Sherlund, and Kamila Sommer, "On the Effect of Student Loans on Access to Homeownership," Finance and Economics Discussion Series 2016-010. Washington, DC: Board of Governors of the Federal Reserve System (2016), accessed March 14, 2017, http://dx.doi.org/10.17016/FEDS.2016.010 .

3. Mike Konczal, "Student Loans Are the New Indentured Servitude," *The Atlantic*, October 12, 2009, accessed May 18, 2017, https://www.theatlantic.com/business/archive/2009/10/student-loans-are-the-new-indentured-servitude/28235/.

4. Sara Goldrick-Rab, *Paying the Price: College Costs, Financial Aid, and the Betrayal of the American Dream* (Chicago: University of Chicago Press, 2016); Robert B. Archibald, *Why Does College Cost So Much?* (New York: Oxford University Press, 2014); Robert Samuels, *Why Public Higher Education Should Be Free: How to Decrease Cost and Increase Quality at American Universities* (New Brunswick, NJ: Rutgers University Press, 2013).

5. Richard Fry, "The Changing Profile of Student Borrowers," Pew Research Center, October 7, 2014, accessed January 1, 2017, http://www.pewsocialtrends.org/2014/10/07/the-changing-profile-of-student-borrowers/.

6. Katie Lobosco, "Students Are Graduating with $30,000 in Loans," CNN Money, October 18, 2016, accessed January 1, 2017, http://money.cnn.com/2016/10/18/pf/college/average-student-loan-debt/.

7. Kim Dancy, "Who Takes Out Parent PLUS Loans Anyway," New America, January 13, 2016, accessed January 1, 2017, https://www.newamerica.org/education-policy/edcentral/parent-plus-loans/.

8. Jonnelle Marte, "It Takes Half as Long to Recoup the Cost of a College Degree Today as It Did in the 1970s," *Washington Post*, September 3, 2014, accessed October 31, 2016, https://www.washingtonpost.com/news/get-there/wp/2014/09/03/it-takes-half-as-long-to-recoup-the-cost-of-a-college-degree-today-as-it-did-in-the-1970s/ .

9. "Is College Worth It," Pew Research Center, May 15, 2011, accessed January 1, 2017, http://www.pewsocialtrends.org/2011/05/15/is-college-worth-it/

10. "Is College Worth It? Goldman Sachs Says Maybe Not," CNN Money, December 9, 2015, accessed January 1, 2017, http://money.cnn.com/2015/12/09/news/economy/college-not-worth-it-goldman/.

11. Jaison R. Abel and Richard Deitz, "Do the Benefits of College Still Outweigh the Costs?" SSRN Scholarly Paper, Rochester, NY: Social Science Research Network, August 1, 2014. https://papers.ssrn.com/abstract=2477864.

12. Louise Bunce, Amy Baird, and Sian E. Jones, "The Student-as-Consumer Approach in Higher Education and Its Effects on Academic Performance," *Studies in Higher Education*, January 14, 2016, doi: 10.1080/03075079.2015.1127908.

13. David Soles, "College Benefits Not Just Economic," *Kansas*, accessed April 24, 2017, http://www.kansas.com/opinion/opn-columns-blogs/article1025628.html.

14. Camille L. Ryan and Kurt Bauman, "Education Attainment in the United States 2015," accessed May 18, 2017, https://www.census.gov/content/dam/Census/library/publications/2016/demo/p20-578.pdf.

15. "Nontraditional Undergraduates / Definitions and Data," National Center for Education Statistics, accessed May 4, 2017, https://nces.ed.gov/pubs/web/97578e.asp

16. Neera Tanden and Matt James, "U.S. Education Must Keep Up with China's, India's Bold Programs," accessed May 19, 2017, https://www.usnews.com/opinion/articles/2012/08/22/us-education-must-keep-up-with-chinas-indias-bold-programs?int=opinion-rec.

17. William J. Bennett and David Wilezol, *Is College Worth It?* (Nashville, TN: Thomas Nelson, 2013).

18. Jeffrey J. Selingo, *There Is Life After College: What Parents and Students Should Know About Navigating School to Prepare for the Jobs of Tomorrow* (New York: William Morrow, 2016), 32.

19. Jon Marcus and Center on Higher Education Reform (CHER) American Enterprise Institute for Public Policy Research (AEI), "Students' Futures as Investments: The Promise and Challenges of Income-Share Agreements. AEI Series on Private Financing in Higher Education," American Enterprise Institute for Public Policy Research, March 1, 2016. American Enterprise Institute for Public Policy Research, 1150 Seventeenth Street NW, Washington, DC 20036. Tel: 202-862-5800; Fax: 202-862-7177; Website: http://www.aei.org .

Chapter Two

What Happens When You Major for Money?

The Guild Mind-set versus an (Inter)Disciplinary Mentality

Heather's parents never attended college, but since she's going, they have high expectations of her. She is an ambitious eighteen-year-old from the Midwest. Heather's mother and father expect her to major in something practical like computer science and get a good job upon graduation. They are keenly aware of the challenges facing women in STEM fields but have encouraged her to persist despite hints that Heather has very high interests and abilities in sculpting.

Her family believes that a degree in computer science will provide access to the high-salaried club of computer programmers, the same way her father had done during the tech boom of the 1990s. He was a self-taught computer programmer and managed to land a good job without the degree. Despite her parents' wishes, Heather hinted that she was still more interested in studying art than computers.

Heather is overjoyed when she receives a letter of acceptance to Somewhere University. Since her parents are paying all the costs, Heather feels the need to defer her love for sculpture to focus on earning a degree in computer science. After all, programming is a clear path to a job. Her father insists that she can make decent money upon graduation if she focuses on a more practical major like computer science and buckles down to graduate early.

Heather's father is well meaning, but his current experiences in the workforce and understanding of the practicality of certain types of college degrees as a one-way ticket to the middle class do not reflect the complexity of the world Heather lives in. The question is not whether Heather should major in sculpture or computer science but rather how she can combine both. Heather's workplace requires college credentials, technical skills, and creative abilities.

In this chapter, we explore how the view of college as an investment prevents Heather's parents and those like them from understanding several important truths that shape the reality of their child's world. American society has given students a scripted path for education—not just in college but in elementary, middle, and high school. The messaging has been consistent: go to college, get an education, earn a degree, and make money.

The problem with this is that students have not been given an opportunity to explore for themselves. Students have been taught to learn for the test, get good grades, do community service, and participate in band, dance, or a sport activity, so much so that it has become a checklist of prerequisites of a life without true meaning of reflection on what these activities mean on a personal level.

We suggest rethinking the college diploma as more than a receipt or a ticket to a job. We explore strategies to help students think about college as a guided curation of educational experiences rather than an obstacle to entering the workplace and earning money. To achieve this mind-set requires a reckoning with three common misconceptions illustrated in Heather's story.

1. Heather's parents falsely equate practicality with profitability and misunderstand the distinction between higher education and career training.
2. Heather's father uncritically substitutes his experiences in a specific moment in the past with her prospects for the future.
3. Heather's parents believe that her personal aptitude, ambition, and interest have no role to play in her immediate college success, future career, or expected earnings.

Collectively, the chapter examines why these three warped views of higher education, based in a narrow understanding of college as an investment, can actually harm Heather's ability to achieve the very goals she has in mind.

HOW TO CRITICALLY INVEST IN A MAJOR

Heather's story is a familiar one to thousands of families across the country. Since the 1970s, the notion of a college diploma as the entry ticket to a particularly secure middle-class job is no longer valid. The medieval time of guilds where young apprentices worked under masters in associations for mutual aid and were protected from external competition has long passed. Yet a kernel of the idea that a college degree is a fail-safe that will protect students from the volatility of the global marketplace remains.

Additionally, often those who view college as an investment think of higher education, particularly the acquisition of certain technical or professional degrees, as an initiation into a hierarchy of knowledge and labor that is completely protected from disruption in the marketplace. In the early 2000s, the most coveted guilds have included computer scientists, engineers, nurses, chemists, and accountants. This was a marked shift from the guilds of previous decades that elevated the role of physicians, lawyers, and educators.

To some extent this ranking of guilds with status had been present for quite some time. What has changed is the social stigma associated with those who do decent and profitable work that does not require a college degree. By going to college, in the past one learned a useful skill set and, in doing so, gained access to a thirty-year career that was protected until retirement. This notion of a guilded, college-educated middle class no longer exists.[1]

A study by Bourdabat (2009) reveals the complexity of the selection of college majors and the shortcomings of a perspective that uses economic means in a guild mentality. When students decide to major based on future monetary returns this sets up a fundamentally dishonest relationship between college and students. Students are resentful when market conditions change and their degree is no longer in high demand, and men and women often make this decision differently. Very few people can predict exactly what market conditions will exist in four years—these expectations are well beyond the abilities of most experts—but it is possible to outline future expectations based on current trends.

Not only are students faced with the prospects of unstable careers but in some of the most volatile of industries, prospects of employment may evaporate before graduation. Many highly technical fields face rapidly shifting certification requirements or worse as technological advancement becomes obsolete much more quickly than at any time prior. Still, students and parents have continued to believe that the possession of a degree or a particular major provides complete protection from these uncertainties.

Much of the recent scrutiny facing the liberal arts and the humanities has been based in this thinking. In the last decades of the twentieth century, the patiently plodding disciplines of the humanities have been outpaced with lightning speed by the relevance of more trade- and professional-oriented fields. However, a college degree, even in high-demand sectors, does not provide permanent insurance against unemployment. A reckoning is coming.

The Great Recession of 2008 demonstrated that highly skilled college graduates from a variety of the so-called professional fields found themselves out of work at rates comparable to those of graduates with liberal arts majors. In addition to this fact, according to the U.S. Census Bureau, 74 percent of those who have a bachelor's degree in a STEM (science, technology, engineering, and math) field were not employed in STEM occupations but were in sales and management.[2] Fears of unemployment and underemployment that parents and students have often attributed to particular degrees is a powerful but misdirected motivator.[3]

In other words, the problem is not with the selection of the major per se but rather the investment logic of specialized jobs requiring a highly technical skill set. The issue here is not that English majors can't get engineering jobs but that students increasingly must have a complex interdisciplinary skill set to meet the ever-changing demands of a global marketplace. Students must choose majors that not only credentialize them but that also prepare them with a mind-set for constant growth and the ability to think quantitatively and creatively.[4]

History has taught us that today's computer science majors may become tomorrow's shorthand specialists. Shorthand and stenography were once highly sought after career skills for administrative assistants but have been replaced by new technologies and practices. The decline of specialized training in these skills reminds us that just because a particular job skill set is in high demand now does not mean that it will remain so indefinitely. Globalization has accelerated the process of making noncritical or creative skills redundant, and educational choices must reflect this rapid pace of change.

The millennials were the first college-educated generation since World War II to face diminishing returns in income and employment prospects.[5] They were not the first generation to be asked to sacrifice their muse for the pursuit of wages but are unique in that they were forced to risk large sums of money to invest in education for an uncertain future.

Investment in a college education will provide a student more protection than none at all but a degree is no longer protection from the fiercely competitive global marketplace. Remember, as we discussed earlier, students born after 1980 are expected to change jobs up to nine times and careers several times during their lifetime.[6] The selection of majors must reflect this reality and a whole host of other factors in addition to earnings.[7]

Most important, college-educated students can no longer hope to enter a "guild" of workers that rely on credentials and group expertise alone. Focusing on narrow fields of technical expertise often comes at the expense of developing broader-base skills that are transferable to other domains.[8] As Thomas Friedman predicted in 2007, the integrative role of liberal arts amidst other emerging fields would be the defining factor of success in the disruptive economies of the future. He was right.[9]

The ability of workers in the skilled trades to collectively bargain has declined. So has the "worth" of a college degree as protection from instability in the marketplace. Educators, policymakers, and parents have responded by drilling down the idea of "something more practical," but this strategy has failed to protect college grads from global changes since students often compete with graduates from abroad with even more specialized backgrounds.

The development of critical thinking, effective writing, interpersonal social skills, and global intercultural competency tends to be overlooked in degree choices. Parents have often failed to consider that the competitive edge of American students is no longer "in the guild" with the credential itself. Graduates who are thriving in today's economy have learned how to bring together multiple and unrelated approaches in creative ways to address a problem.

For example, new careers in game design, the culinary arts explosion, and the growth of opportunities in nursing have also demonstrated that students who are doing best are bringing together diverse skill sets from across the college curriculum. In the start-up culture that characterized the early 2000s, college students are innovatively revisiting the humanities and social sciences. They have integrated new technological approaches to old questions. The result has been an astonishing explosion of industry and the remaking of the Internet into Web 2.0.

DEGREE WHEELS OF INTELLECTUAL STAGNATION

Have you ever watched a hamster run on a wheel? The hamster runs without any real progress or meaningful pathway. It runs as if internally programmed to go in one direction without exploring, learning, and growing. The hamster on the wheel sees only two choices—to stand still or to run. Similar to the hamster, college students face this same challenge of stagnancy and unidirectional thinking. The wheel movement gives the illusion that evolution is taking place, but they only appear to be going forward.

Perhaps the majority of American students in college face a similar dilemma. Like Heather and our hamster, many students feel that by merely enrolling in college, majoring, and matriculating, they are achieving. This false notion of achievement and security by stationary motion is detrimental to the American educational system. Instead of asking questions about deep learning and mastery, parents and students merely focus on maintaining the illusion of forward motion even if there is no intellectual progress.

From elementary school onward, students, parents, and policymakers have been trained to emphasize external validation as primary evidence of intellectual development. This comes with certain costs. While external measurements are necessary, an overreliance on these crude instruments has often distracted from the actual experience of learning itself.

This way of thinking often accompanies an investment outlook that parents and students bring to the college experience—by bubbling in multiple-choice tests, passing on from one class to the next, and grasping for degree after degree without ever really moving intellectually from the place they began. This intellectual inertia causes significant problems as students enter college because it has become so ingrained in their thinking toward learning and their expectations of education. The problem is not the investment mindset per se but the attitude that students have toward learning itself.

Heather's father has this mentality because of the unique challenges his generation faced, but today such an approach is not only outdated but can be very expensive for students. Each individual pathway is not the same. We learn differently. We work differently. We engage differently. And, without understanding oneself it is difficult to create that pathway.

Most students who enter college do not have an understanding of what they really like to do. Students have been given script after script about what fields are most popular in the monetary sense but know far too little about themselves and the world they will inhabit to make a well-informed decision.

- So, how do we help students develop both personally and intellectually as they go through the educational process so it connects with their career interests?
- With such a structured educational program with activities, how do they find out their passion?
- Most important, how do they understand who they are?

PASSION AND IDENTITY: THE CORE OF INTELLECTUAL LEARNING

We suggest rethinking the college diploma as something more than a receipt or a ticket to a job. Parents and advisors must rethink how they support the role of education and how to support students finding their life's purpose and intellectual identity.

One's identity begins forming in the mother's womb. Every emotion that she feels is internalized by the unborn child. When the child is given a name, it defines the core being of who he or she is because of its meaning and significance to their family.

In Akan culture in Ghana, a person's name is rooted in the familial identity, culture, and character that is instilled in the child. After the child is born, he or she is kept indoors for eight days; then commences the naming ceremony, where family gathers to celebrate the new addition to the family. The first name given is based on the child's birth day of the week. Then, the child is provided a formal name that is the heart of his or her identity and connects to an ancestral clan. Typically, this name has deeper meaning and defines the child's purpose in the world.

Americans would do well to learn from the lessons of the Akan. In American society, children are often subscribed to a list of activities that help them become well-rounded individuals. They focus on the academic experience and then branch off into a range of activities, such as dance, playing instruments, sports, joining a club, and community service. Student schedules are often packed with stuff without room for reflection on self and relationships to others. Far too often, college majors are developed in silos from other disciplines and further contribute to the intellectual and social isolation of student learners.

By the time they reach college, students may have some idea of what careers they want to pursue, but this is often based on vague ideas of expected earnings or parental pressures. Students seldom select majors aligned with true knowledge and exploration of oneself. Colleges have a vast amount of resources to help students with this but can only be effective when students utilize them early and often through their educational journey. Parents, advisors, and students must substitute being busy with engaged and efficacious learning.

In college, offices of student life and engagement provide students with an abundance of activities around leadership development, community service, alternative spring breaks, and so forth. Unfortunately, students and parents often do not see the value of these experiences in relation to their major or future careers. How do we develop a holistic model where parents and students students explore, experience, and engage in self and future career aspirations?

A MAJOR IS MORE THAN A MEAL TICKET

What if Heather and her parents had begun her college journey with another approach that matched her identity, purpose, and passion? What if Heather's parents viewed college as an investment in her identity? Students who major in areas that they are personally interested and invested in are more motivated to achieve higher levels of learning and impact other areas of their lives.[10] Parents and advisors must pursue experiences that help students explore these areas so they can find out where their true passion lies.

At Somewhere University, it is not so much *what* Heather majors in but *how* she does it. In other words, Heather's major is less important than the mind-set and learning strategies that she adopts to align her intellectual passion with demands in the marketplace. Conventional wisdom has taught that every passion or hobby need not be a major. However, the central lesson of college need not be that students must dismantle fervent interests for gainful employment—the best colleges find ways to merge both.

Heather's Somewhere University is a four-year public institution nationally known for its prestigious engineering program. The school is bursting at the seams with students, and the retention rate has always been around 90 percent because of its top-notch faculty, experiential learning center, mentoring programs, and flexible degree options. Approximately 30 percent of the students are international and, of the remaining student population, 20 percent are from underrepresented groups (e.g., African American, Latino, etc.). Every student in the program has either a faculty or staff mentor that has expertise in the field of engineering.

Initially, the curricular plan allowed little room for courses outside of engineering. However, over the last decade, Somewhere University became one of the best national models for interdisciplinary work and experiential engagement. Heather found supportive faculty and staff who have helped her navigate the engineering curriculum but also encourage collaborations and exposure to the arts and the humanities. Heather has a diversified skill set that makes her highly engaged and highly sought after in the global marketplace.

Other innovative models have emerged from engaging the questions about the role of passion, identity, and purpose in the quest for a major. Minerva is a twenty-first-century higher education institution on the cutting edge of holistic, interdisciplinary, and global experiences that allow students to passionately experience and engage in learning. The experience disrupts the guild mentality by focusing on highly adaptive classroom units and dynamic learning environments.

Launched in the fall of 2014, Minerva specializes in students mastering analytical skills, team building, and active learning, through interdisciplinary approaches that promote student engagement. Students who enroll in Minerva will live in seven different cities during the course of study: Buenos Aires, London, Berlin, Seoul, Taipei, Hyderabad, and San Francisco. Minerva provides precisely the kinds of engaged, interdisciplinary, and experiential approaches that make the investment in learning more meaningful for students and parents.

Aside from being a study-abroad haven, there are no lectures allowed and all classes are facilitated through online learning, with pedagogy steeped in high-impact practices that challenge students to work on project-based initiatives. The digital platform allows students and professors mobility and access from anywhere in the world. Ben Nelson, the founder, states that "Minerva is structured around true-life application and preparing students for jobs in the real world."[11]

FROM MASTERY TO META LEARNING

One unfortunate result of viewing college as purely an economic investment is that students approach learning with the idea that it is something instantly imbued and permanently achieved that leads directly to practical application. Many students have this view because for twelve years of their prior education, they have been taught in an environment that prioritizes fixed and immediate outcomes. Colleges often contribute to this fallacy that mastery occurs at the end of course by the way learning is assessed and grades are assigned.

Most educators understand that learning is not a linear process. Students progress and regress, they make gains and lose them. They learn everything and forget it all. The hope is that at the end of a particular period, students will have learned enough that somethings sticks. What does stick most often is not what colleges and policymakers are most interested in measuring. Those moments often occur outside of the classroom, sometimes without professors, but are profoundly the result of higher forms of self-directed inquiry and reflection that are difficult to replicate outside of college.

Instead of focusing on a particular future point in time, students and parents would benefit greatly if they developed a longer-term and more procedural outlook on learning. Learning is not completed at a particular point in time but is a lifelong process. The goal of education is not to arrive at a point of completion but to transform ways of seeing and interacting in the world that students can continue to build upon after graduating for the rest of their lives.

In order to get to this type of approach, students need to focus much less on mastery of concepts and emphasize *meta learning*. Meta learning is a complex field of cognitive psychology that emerged in the late 1970s. At the core of meta learning is the idea that humans are more effective learners when they give adequate attention to the process of learning itself in addition to the content. A period of reflection after using this approach provides students with an opportunity to unpack ideas from the course content that could eventually turn into a project or invention. The concept of theory to practice is essential to developing meta learning.

In the past, when novices wanted to embark on a new trade they would become apprentices of a so-called master. It is no coincidence that this form of learning is nearly ubiquitous in every culture in the world. From the medieval squires who have been romanticized in Western literature to African and Asian neophytes, the mentoring relationship is the most effective relationship not only in transferring knowledge but also in developing the mind-set of in-depth learning.

In times past, the notions of learning were never separate from making a living. Students saw firsthand how their masters were able to eke out a living from their trades and learned the complex relationship between knowledge and praxis years before venturing out on their own.

As the modern world shifted increasingly to quantify and to measure only certain types of cognitive abilities, this broader notion of a somewhat symbiotic relationship between a teacher and a student, between living and learning, was lost. Educators became more interested in measuring intellectual *capability*. However, the assessment of capability at one fixed point in time is not a good predictor of future ability and aptitude.

SAT and ACT test scores are one of the primary assessments used to determine if a student is a good fit for an institution, along with high school grades, an essay, recommendation letters, and engagement in activities presented in a résumé format. Highly selective institutions often require interviews for evaluation purpose, but how does one actually measure a student's cognitive ability without understanding the whole student?

RANKING THE PRICE OF MENTORING RELATIONSHIPS

Another outcome of viewing college as purely an economic investment is that students severely neglect the importance of nurturing long-term relationships with academic experts. Since mentoring relationships have been such an important part of higher education it is surprising that most collegiate ranking schemes fail to account for this aspect of learning. A mentor is someone with wisdom, experience, and expertise who serves as a guide and/or teacher to a person.

Some tools score student-to-professor ratios or the availability of academic counseling as a factor in their assessment. However, no tools exist that explore perhaps the most important component—one-to-one mentoring relationships. The role of the apprenticeship and its modern form, known as the assistantship, is usually found throughout schools with graduate programs.

At the baccalaureate level, students at many public institutions will often reach the upper divisions of their course requirements without actually being taught by a full-time instructor. This has occurred for a variety of reasons. More students are taking online courses in the lower division, finishing up courses in introductory math and literature to save money before moving on to more specialized courses in a particular major.

For the vast majority of students, the decision was made for them as higher-educational institutions have slashed the number of full-time faculty. This phenomenon has been discussed at great detail in a variety of other recent works, but it is important for us to consider here particularly as it relates to the student-faculty mentoring relationship.

Part-time faculty are often great instructors—they are energetic, they are motivated, and they love the subject matter. However, since they are sorely underpaid and are considered transient employees, it is very difficult for students to develop long-term sustaining relationships. There are a few part-time instructors who stay in their roles for longer periods of time but are often overlooked as potential mentors to students.

The absence of these types of nurturing relationships—whether from an increasing number of courses delivered online, growing proportions of student-to-faculty ratios, or inaccessibility to full-time faculty—impacts the value of the college degree. If students have only a credential with little guided mentoring and meta-learning skills that so often develop within these relationships, they graduate with a degree but within a few years that degree becomes merely paper.

The rapidly evolving nature of the knowledge economy requires constant learning and networking within an ever-changing intellectual environment. A mentor is needed to help students navigate this deluge of knowledge. The norms and cultures of each discipline rapidly change and, without the support of content experts who have an understanding of the intellectual landscape, recent graduates are destined to become dinosaurs.

When assessing the value of your college degree, students, parents, and advisors need to pay more attention to the role of mentoring relationships. When students attend orientation, they must ask about the student-to-professor ratio but also about the percentage of part-time faculty. Institutions that are not investing in full-time faculty are not investing in academic mentoring, and you should make your decision with that in mind. Furthermore, students must be equally critical of ranking systems for the best colleges and universities that fail to incorporate these criteria in their assessments.

THE CURRICULAR COSTS OF AN INVESTMENT MENTALITY

In addition to the mentality of students and relationships with faculty being impacted by the investment approach to higher education, as college bureaucracies absorb this impetus the historical diversity of the college curricula has been severely limited.

Students are seldom provided the opportunity to explore and creatively engage connections between disparate fields of knowledge and disciplines. The efficiency-oriented agenda of the career-focused student attempts to streamline the breadth of the curriculum and be intellectually segregated as possible. There have been negative outcomes associated with these approaches, but colleges continue to yield to the market demand for these shortcuts.

Consequently, the majority of students are unable to understand or even cultivate the desire to understand the multiple applications of diverse, interconnected, overlapping, and often contradictory disciplines and bodies of knowledge. Students understand job training but are not afforded enough time or opportunities in college to develop competencies that may be applicable across a variety of careers.

Table 2.1, Guild Jobs and Interdisciplinary Career Paths, shows students which core competencies align with their major and career paths. The table provides a context of the types of career paths that students can take while developing core competencies.

Most colleges don't do well at helping students find these competency-based connections between majors, careers, and intersections of course-level knowledge because they are organized with the exact opposite purpose. Furthermore, the rapid-paced temperament of the current college crisis affords little opportunity for these slow-learning types of arrangements and experiential opportunities. Courses and majors are often viewed as completely separate units, and faculty rarely collaborate because they are financed in competition with each other.

In other words, biologists and historians or thespians and computer scientists seldom collaborate in large universities because they are focused on conducting research in their field of study. Furthermore, you would be less likely to see a theater professor collaborate with a computer scientist or a business colleague because American society has created a script for each field of study and they don't go outside of it.

This may seem to be a minor challenge but it has real consequences for students and parents because this is not how the future economies will work or even how they are currently working. There seems to be a disconnect within higher education on how departments can complement one another and assist students with broadening their areas of expertise and skill sets.

Students who plan on going to medical school to become physicians are often advised to stick to the curriculum and volunteer within their area of study. But what is often lacking is the opportunity to develop interpersonal, cross-disciplinary, and cross-cultural communication skills that will strengthen the patient-doctor relationship. We learn not to confirm what we already know but to prepare for opportunities of which we are not aware.

The investment mentality has undermined these opportunities and indirectly led to a cannibalizing of the curricula. There is an ever-dwindling number of intellectual options for students. Students are often told to avoid majoring in any subject that has *studies*, *liberal*, *arts*, or *humanities* in the title. This is unfortunate because many of these content areas not only provide key insights to areas that are ripe for intellectual inquiry but also provide deep analysis of historical or contemporary problems that are ripe for entrepreneurial activity.

For example, the STEM fields and other related disciplines provide students with a specific set of skills for their highly specialized careers but often fail to effectively create interconnections with liberal arts departments. There

Table 2.1. Guild Jobs and Interdisciplinary Career Paths

Major	Expected Job	Unexpected Career	Core Competencies
Computer Science	Programmer	Entrepreneur	Logic Sequential Design Analytical Thinking Concentration Detail Oriented Problem-Solving
Business	Sales Manager	Nonprofit Administrator	Time Management Skills Interpersonal Skills Problem-Solving Communication Analytical Skills
Communications	Public Relations Specialist	Consultant	Knowledge of History Interpersonal Skills Organizational Skills Problem-Solving
History	Teacher	Program Director	Research Skills Analytical Skills Problem-Solving Communication Skills
Economics	Economist	Financial Aid Advisor	Quantitative Skills Analytical Thinking Writing Critical Thinking Skills Detailed-Oriented
Psychology	Psychologist	Fitness Coach	Observational Skills Patience Communication Problem-Solving Trustworthiness Analytical
Chemical Engineering	Chemist	Creator of Skin Products	Problem-Solving Ingenuity Quantitative Skills Creativity Analytical Skills
Biology	Biologist	Social Worker	Technical Skills Observational Skills Analytical Skills Critical Thinking

Nursing	Nurse	Researcher	Emotional Stability Detailed-Oriented Organizational Skills Physical Stamina
English	Teacher	Ghost Writer	Critical Thinking Resourcefulness Interpersonal Skills Speaking Writing

is no incentive to do so within many colleges and universities. However, in the so-called real world these STEAM (STEM + Arts) collaborations have been very effective and quite profitable.

Often, advocates of professional-oriented or STEM-quarantined curricula argue against a broad-based liberal arts education and especially the humanities as a waste of time and money. From a student's perspective, these courses and certain kinds of liberal arts majors often provide competencies that continue to increase in economic and personal value over time despite initial perspectives about their worth upon graduation and during the time of enrollment.

Furthermore, it costs colleges and universities less money to offer courses in the humanities—a field constantly berated as irrelevant and a bad choice for students seeking to make the most of their tuition dollars—than courses in engineering, technology, and lab-based sciences. Administrators discovered a long time ago that many courses in the humanities subsidize the development of other high-cost fields since students all pay the same for their tuition regardless of what they choose to major in.[12]

Courses in the humanities often provide a foundation of skills for critical thinking and self-directed learning that advance the goals of more specialized majors, which seldom happens in the reverse. The college experience allows students to engage new ideas and perspectives through interactions with people and subjects they never would interact with or invest in otherwise. The cost of college subsidizes broader transactions that have a lateral impact throughout American society and the world at large.

CONCLUSION

To fully benefit from the investment of dollars in college, students need a breadth of intellectual experiences, opportunities to develop personally meaningful insights and connections between courses and their personal lives, and mutually beneficial long-term relationships with academic experts. Education is essential for continual learning and development. John Dewey

(1897) states that "education is the fundamental method of social progress and reform."[13]

How many students are like Heather and the hamster in the wheel, running intently and focused on one direction but oblivious to opportunities surrounding her? The most transformational educational experiences take place in unconventional ways—through action, adequate reflection, and guided interaction.

Heather's dilemma frames the challenges that many contemporary students face. As if the prospects of attending a completely new educational environment were not unsettling enough, they now must also contend with outdated modes of learning and demands of their parents to make economic and personal sacrifices to the most intellectually important things about them. Incoming students understand much more than their parents that college is no longer what it used to be—passion and creativity must be part of the learning process.

Savvy students also understand that the acquisition of a good education no longer guarantees a job, a good salary, or a stable financial future. At this juncture, students are assessing whether the college experience is worth it, and those who do pursue a college education are deeply critical of degree programs and curricular arrangements that do little to speak to their current concerns or economic futures.

Ironically, colleges have been reluctant to address these concerns in any meaningful way. Most universities are content to continue to offer courses in the humanities and arts while significantly underfunding them. On the other hand, very few universities have the resources to completely rework the institutional model based on cutting-edge technologies and the most recent market innovations.

The college governance structure and institutional organization is based on a very old model that was not designed to endure the rapid change in global economic systems and culture. It is very difficult to change the institutional culture of established educational institutions unless they were designed to accompany and embrace such changes.

The sad fact is that the guild mentality that so many people expect from college is exactly how colleges continue to present themselves, a bit of deceptive advertising in the current age. The good news is that there are innovative models emerging that reach back to the past to provide a holistic education while also reaching to the future to assume much nimbler organizational structures and curricula innovations that are responsive to rapidly changing needs that the global economy presents.

It is incumbent that students challenge the assumptions of both their parents and outmoded educational institutions about the role that college degrees play. Students must increasingly learn to put course content and degrees into dialogue with each other even as colleges and universities continue to make such opportunities difficult to have.

Action Steps

If the current approach to college as an investment tends to emphasize technical mastery over passionate exploration, credentialization over the development of cross-disciplinary competency, individualization over collaboration, and guild-thinking instead of meta-thinking learning, what can students, parents, and advisors do to respond?

1. Pause for a moment, reflect on an experience that you have had in your lifetime that you have learned something from. What was that transformational moment?
2. How a degree will provide a return on investment (ROI) is even more difficult to measure if you are not sure what your professional goals are. It is crucial that students spend time understanding their abilities, aptitudes, and areas early on in their educational journey, preferably before college. What are your professional and personal goals? And, how do they align with your strengths?
3. Before you start looking at colleges/universities, write out a general outline of the fields of study that you would like to pursue. You should have at least ten on one page.
4. Peruse the course catalog and courses offered at your prospective college. What courses and intellectual excursions does it provide that expand your perspectives on what is possible within your intended or current field of study? Think of the most important classes and professors as extended internships rather than spectator sports. How will these courses continue to provide insight after the course has ended? In five years? Ten years? Twenty-five years?
5. Develop independent projects and applications of course content that rely on the expertise of your professors to advance your personal goals and interests. What questions do you have about how certain ideas could be combined with other areas of intellectual inquiry or developed beyond the answers that are readily provided?
6. Focus on requesting honest assessment and feedback from your professor and forget about arguing over grades. Develop a long-term relationship with your professor as a mentor. This is one of the most valuable and effective returns on the money you are spending on higher education. Finding a suitable mentor is much more important than arguing over minuses and pluses in an era when grades are grossly inflated.

7. When you attend an open house or orientation ask about the student-to-professor ratio but also ask about the percentage of part-time to full-time faculty. Determine whether you will receive or are receiving the academic and mentoring support you need with these proportions. Can you make a choice where your dollars would be better invested in more opportunities with close collaboration and mentorships with subject matter experts in your field?

NOTES

1. Christopher Newfield, *Unmaking the Public University: The Forty-Year Assault on the Middle Class* (Boston: Harvard University Press, 2011), 13.

2. "STEM Crisis or STEM Surplus? Yes, and Yes," Monthly Labor Review: U.S. Bureau of Labor Statistics, accessed January 31, 2017. https://www.bls.gov/opub/mlr/2015/article/stem-crisis-or-stem-surplus-yes-and-yes.htm.

3. "How Do Young People Choose College Majors?," accessed September 18, 2016, http://citeseerx.ist.psu.edu/viewdoc/download?doi=10.1.1.606.4138&rep=rep1&type=pdf.

4. "Hunting for Soft Skills, Companies Scoop Up English Majors," accessed October 31, 2016, http://finance.yahoo.com/news/hunting-soft-skills-companies-scoop-140100691.html.

5. Leah McGrath Goodman, "U.S. Millennial College Graduates: Young, Educated, and Jobless," accessed May 19, 2017, http://www.newsweek.com/2015/06/05/millennial-college-graduates-young-educated-jobless-335821.html.

6. Laura Donovan, "Why Millennials Change Jobs," accessed May 17, 2017, https://www.attn.com/stories/1602/why-millennials-change-jobs.

7. Anthony Patrick Carnevale, Jeff Strohl, and Michelle Melton, *What's It Worth?: The Economic Value of College Majors* (Washington, DC: Georgetown University Center on Education and the Workforce, 2011).

8. Bradford Holmes, "Hone the Top 5 Soft Skills Every College Student Needs," accessed on May 17, 2017, https://www.usnews.com/education/blogs/college-admissions-playbook/2014/05/12/hone-the-top-5-soft-skills-every-college-student-needs.

9. Thomas Friedman, *The World Is Flat: A Brief History of the Twenty-First Century* (New York: Macmillan, 2005), 316–18.

10. Ulrich Schiefele, "Interest, Learning, and Motivation," *Educational Psychologist* 26, no. 3–4 (June 1, 1991): 299–323. doi:10.1080/00461520.1991.9653136.

11. "Tech Entrepreneur Ben Nelson Heralds Last Hurrah for Uni Lecture," *The Australian*, August 17, 2016.

12. Lee J. Cuba, Nancy E. Jennings, Suzanne Lovett, and Joseph Swingle, *Practice for Life* (Cambridge, MA: Harvard University Press, 2016).

13. John Dewey, *Democracy and Education* (North Chelmsford, MA: Courier Corporation, 2004/1916).

Chapter Three

Why Are American Universities So Expensive?

Getting What You Pay For

Todd wants to pursue a career in website development. His father is an alumnus of a private highly selective liberal arts college named Eclectic College. Todd is considering attending his father's alma mater but he knows that the tuition is high there, especially when compared to some of the other schools on his shortlist. He narrows his decisions to Eclectic College, Green College, and Degreedy University.

Todd is drawn to the other schools not because of their computer science programs but because they both have his major and offer excellent extracurricular offerings for student life. Eclectic College has tiny dorm rooms but has a new technology annex and graphic design studios. Green College is known primarily for academics. Degreedy University has the best living arrangements—it boasts resort-like dorms, a lazy river, and climbing walls.

As Todd reviews each of the glossy fliers and reflects on the campus tours, he begins to consider tuition costs seriously for the first time. Green College is 50 percent cheaper than the other options. Eclectic is the most expense. Degreedy is about 5 percent less than Eclectic. It seems that the best option would be to invest in the school with the best amenities. Since Degreedy costs less per year than Eclectic it seems like a good deal to Todd.

Todd thinks that the amenities offered on campus life reveal the quality of the education that he will receive. The better the facilities are, the better the deal he is getting. Todd has never met any of the faculty or staff at any of the universities or looked at the graduation rates and future earnings of recent graduates. Still, he can't imagine himself attending a college without any creature comforts and especially Green College—they don't even have a football team.

Todd's story is a familiar one to thousands of families across the country. Since the 1990s, colleges have been engaging in an amenities race to attract students that has significantly raised the cost of higher education. In 1995, $6.1 billion were spent on turning dormitories into lavish apartments, swimming pools, bowling alleys, and quads with plasma televisions with a couple of intramural sports. Today, the investment in amenities has almost tripled, and schools that fail to compete with broad offerings in athletics, student housing, and campus perks find themselves playing second fiddle to more expensive schools.[1]

Todd makes several assumptions about college as an investment that will have a long-term impact on his educational experiences and economic circumstances long after he graduates.

- First, he fails to distinguish the difference in the value provided by four-year colleges and community colleges based on his particular area of interest and career goals.
- Second, he views tuition as a primary factor in determining whether to attend a school without adequately considering the difference in the prestige of the institutions and the long-term value of the degree.
- Last, he allows amenities to distract him from other more important criteria that factor into his educational costs and that will have long-term consequences on his economic future.

Sadly, these decisions that Todd faces have real impacts on students. Many make one of the most important financial decisions of their lives based on bells and whistles that will be worthless after graduation.

Furthermore, Todd would probably be better off majoring in English or Art History as a student at Green College, a private university vested in interdisciplinary and cross-cultural approaches to education. He could pick up courses in web development at a nearby community college or online at a major discount. Green College focuses on five high-impact educational practices, such as study abroad, learning communities, internships, service learning, and global competency.[2]

Attending Green College would give Todd an opportunity to focus on developing an evolving personalized career blueprint, cultivate enriching experiences, and save a lot of money. By paying very high tuition for an expensive liberal arts college like Eclectic, Todd is taking on additional costs that could best be served elsewhere in his educational journey.

There is a widespread perception today that colleges spend most of the money on instruction, but this is not true. Numerous studies have shown that other costs account for a significant portion of how tuition dollars are spent.

The difficulty in finding information about college expenditures and reports on how colleges actually spend student money leaves many students and families in the dark and on the hook for thousands of dollars that may very well not be used in the best interests of Todd or many students like him.

Todd thinks he is getting a bargain at a school with an athletic reputation like Eclectic College but he would more likely be better off at Green College because it dedicates more of its tuition dollars directly to instruction. Todd justifies his selection of Eclectic College based on some marketing gimmicks that foreground college athletics and campus amenities. It is likely that Todd's four-year education at Eclectic college will set him back just under $50,000 per year. Todd would be much better off buying season tickets to his favorite NFL team, purchasing a home in a low-cost-of-living market, and attending Green College.

Most students do not ask questions about the college budget prior to attendance or during attendance that align with their assumptions and expectations about their college investment. They expect their college experiences to naturally align with the money they are spending. They expect that by spending more for things that they want—even if these amenities are superfluous—will translate into the same material successes following graduation.

This kind of reasoning is responsible for a great deal of buyer's remorse amongst many alumni today. The most tragic part of this drama is that students think they are getting a bargain by paying tuition and living like kings and queens, never once questioning how that money is spent and how they will repay it.

Upon graduation, students find that the cost and standard of living that they are accustomed to is far out of balance with what they are confronted with in the so-called real world. As graduates begin to repay student loans for the next twenty to thirty years they must come to terms with a difficult question: Has their borrowed tuition money helped finance stadiums and fancy recreational facilities that have little impact on their academic life and prospects for post-graduation success?

When thinking of the term *investment*, typically Americans think about stock portfolios, U.S. treasury notes, and perhaps rental property, or maybe the dot.com bust of the 1990s or the housing market crash of 2008. By shifting the context to focus on college and understanding the amount of money actually spent on educating students, it helps to understand what they get in return for their time, money, and experiences.

This chapter discusses the ways in which college has been framed as an important part of a student's career growth and professional development. A central argument in this chapter is that the notion that students and parents are "not receiving what they have paid for" is false. Students are receiving exactly what they are paying for, which is often superficial (e.g., college athletics, dorms, rock climbing walls, etc.). Colleges are consumer-driven enterprises and this reality results in educational agendas that are based on immediate gratification. Parents and students must become more savvy about the impact of their spending in driving what colleges spend on.

YOUR COLLEGE FANTASY AND YOUR COLLEGE'S BUDGET

How a particular college spends your tuition dollars may seem to be irrelevant to the broader trajectory of your student's college experience. However, the university's investment of your tuition dollars has a direct connection to your educational experience and your future success. Universities that emphasize spending in the classroom (e.g., hiring full-time faculty, fully staffed student support services, and experiential learning activities) are usually a better selection than universities that prioritize extracurricular sports and noninstructional capital expansion projects.

Dollar for dollar, monies invested in the classroom contribute to lower student-to-professor ratios, which means more opportunities for mentorship, hands-on learning, and collaborative networking. Dollars spent on administrative overhead, noninstructional fees, athletics, etc., all leech the value of your educational spending.

Then the question becomes what aspects of a college experience and costs actually increase one's value in the job market? Does everyone have a fair chance to determine the best use of their money to reap the benefits of their investment?

PRIORITIES IN CONFLICT: STUDENTS GETTING WHAT THEY PAY FOR—SOMETIMES

Popular arguments that students are "not receiving what they are paying for" are also paradoxical. Perhaps the most stunning irony about the crisis of education is that students are receiving exactly what they are paying for. An investor who bets on a stock merely because other people are betting on that stock and sees the value of the stock skyrocket without carefully examining the fundamentals of the market can expect a grand disappointment.

Likewise, students who are voting with their feet and dollars without examining the fundamentals of what education means are in for a surprise. Students who elect to take easy classes, major in less challenging subjects, and flock to doting professors put the entire university system in a position to reward such behavior and contribute to a speculative environment. Universities are not building stadiums and flashy dormitories, preferring the exploitation of adjuncts over tenure-track positions because students don't want them. They are responding to market conditions.

There are several good examples of colleges and universities aligning spending with student expectations. Recently, Spelman College has attempted to address this dilemma by significantly cutting many of the costly and sometimes distracting extracurricular activities on campus. Former president Beverly Tatum chose to pursue wellness programming as a cheaper and more holistic alternative. The emphasis on health and wellness is a better value for the students because it provides lifestyle education that will impact the quality of living over a lifetime rather than entertainment. Choices like these are often not popular among students but provide lower costs and a higher value.

To think of this in terms of a return on investment, if students (investors) choose to put their money toward things that return little value in the long term, who is to blame? As Ginsberg (2013) has argued, professors wield considerably less influence over the entire scenario than the public believes. As many have rightly critiqued the lack of rigor taking place in higher education, we must also note that the professoriate has retreated from engaged teaching and critical evaluation of student skills precisely because students do not prioritize those activities themselves.[3]

The blogosphere is replete with stories of hard-working professors whose efforts to provide honest appraisals of student work have outraged student-customers and brought the rebuff of higher administration. If students are in fact investing in themselves but unwilling to pay for honest appraisals of the worth of their skills in progress, this is a failure not only of the university but of the entire market-oriented approach to higher education. Students and parents must demand a return to an institutional investment in educational excellence.

INVESTING IN INEQUALITY

Media analysts, people in the field of higher education, and policymakers historically have stressed the importance of an education for everyone in America. But what does a *universal higher education policy* mean? Does everyone require or need a college education? If we examine the comments of the majority of our leaders in America, I think the answer would be yes. But not everyone has access to the prerequisite skills or mind-set necessary for such an investment.

At the Millennium Summit in 2000, thousands of world leaders gathered at the UN Millennium Declaration to create eight Millennium Development Goals (MDGs) to assist with the development of basic human rights for individuals globally. One of those goals, number two, challenged each country to increase the number of boys and girls who complete a primary education. A reworking of the role of college as a mandatory milestone will require more Green Colleges and fewer DeGreedy and Eclectic Universities.

- Investing in a nation where every citizen has a college degree means preparing for a future where the *role of college* will be radically different than its historical function.
- Investing in a nation where every citizen has a college degree means preparing for a more *competitive workplace*.

Additionally, the vast majority of students we have encountered over the last decade believe that a college degree is the best route to getting a better-paying job or launching a career. Then the question becomes does a college degree actually increase one's value in the job market? And does everyone have a fair chance to obtain a college education and reap the benefits of its rewards? How are our current investment choices in the amenities-focused college agenda divesting our future wealth and career choices?

Investing in a nation where every citizen has a college degree means rethinking the *college pipeline*. In order for every student who desires it to have access to college, middle schools and high schools would play a fundamentally different role and offer more job training than they currently do. Instead of focusing solely on rudimentary educational skills, we need much more advanced job training and coordination with the labor market.

At the core of this we must ask ourselves a fundamental question about *when* students are capable of determining their career goals. For many Americans, making such serious decisions before eighteen years of age is difficult.

Most of the countries that subsidize or provide universal college education already have such programs in place. For example, Germany provides cooperative opportunities for students and employers and has even developed models for this approach in the United States.

Investing in a nation where every citizen has a college degree means directly addressing *educational inequality*. Simply making college affordable for all will not transform the fundamental economic inequalities in this country. If students are not ready for a college education, the existing arrangement will only be exacerbated by existing inequalities. In order to truly combat educational inequality, we as a society must come to terms with the stigma we associate with different kinds of students and different types of education.

By readily assuming that students of color, particularly black and Latino students, are incapable of educational rigor or that those who pursue careers in the trades are somehow less important than those with white-collar jobs, we make presuppositions about the nature of higher education that undermine our collective economic goals.

At one point in time, education was seen as an avenue whereby one could gain knowledge. Do you remember the saying "Knowledge is power"? We can go back as far as the 1960s civil rights movement where activists were fighting for the right to have an education. Everyone did not have access to a quality education, let alone a college education.

Learning how to read, write, and think critically was more than just getting a better job, but it provided a foundation for powerful movements in history and gave individuals a sense of pride and confidence in themselves. Key turning points in American history include but definitely are not limited to *Brown vs. Board of Education*, the Civil Rights Act, and *Grutter vs. Bollinger*, each having had a connection to access to higher education for underrepresented students. Even though we have had massive movements for equality, access for underrepresented students continues to remain an issue in higher education.

Many times success has been defined as creating the perfect formula in terms of preparing for career and family life. But it does not necessarily work that way for everyone. Over the last several years college has become a booming business that caters to the ideal that success equals a degree and that a degree leads to a great job. There is no one model that fits each student who arrives on college campus for success. However, we have seen some strategies that have led to the success of some college students. Before we go into this, let me define what we mean by "success in college."

Success is the ability to achieve a goal that further promotes personal and professional growth towards one's purpose or calling, along with the continual development of specific skill sets, such as leadership, intercultural competency, community building, and the ability to create a vision that is articulated into more opportunities for the greater global community.

When thinking of *success in college* there are various perspectives from which this phrase can be defined—from that of the parent, the student, admissions counselors, professors, senior level administrators, and the American public. For the purpose of this book, we define success in college from the perspective of the faculty, the student, and middle-level administrators in the field of higher education.

ADVISING FOR THE GLOBAL MARKETPLACE OF IDEAS

As our society continues to grow globally, it is even more essential that we prepare students to work in this market through the development of cultural literacy and competency. As an advisor, faculty, and success coach, I have seen increasing numbers of students leave college without the necessary intellectual, social, and cultural capital to succeed in a global marketplace of ideas. So, what does this mean—intellectual, social, and cultural capital?

It means possessing a cache of competencies that go beyond merely defining diversity and inclusion. We need to provide students with opportunities for interactions that build on effective communication and social skills across cultural boundaries. This is not just about learning how to write, speak, and read multiple languages but about valuing cultural traditions and developing a mutual respect for others' perspectives. Study away/abroad experiences serve as one mode of increasing cultural competency through the lens of others.

Being able to walk a mile in someone else's shoes helps students to develop their own self-efficacy and prepare them to work anywhere in the world. These experiences were central to our personal career choices, which we could never have known at the time, but they have also been important to many of the students we have advised who could not articulate the full economic significance of these experiences at the time.

Norms of the American middle class have changed with our expectations of a college degree. We are rapidly approaching an era where college degrees will be something akin to the high school diploma. The distinguishing factor will no longer be the credential per se but rather the totality of the experiences surrounding the degree. To "invest" in middle-class ambitions means more than being able to pay for a college degree but also to invest in a variety of experiences that reflect a well-rounded education in a global sense.

One particularly defeatist inhibition of viewing college as an economic investment is that it focuses on purely individualistic measures of success in a fiercely competitive global environment. How do we prepare students to be more entrepreneurial and interdisciplinary and get them to think beyond the narrow confines of their degree to address the complex, multifaceted problems of the real world? There needs to be an interconnection of fields of study (e.g., curricula for a degree in medicine would also include practical courses in psychology so that an appropriate bedside manner could be learned).

CONCLUSION

In an age where colleges are consumer-oriented, buyers must beware. Effective advisement must provide holistic perspectives on experiential and nonlinear benefits that go beyond a transactional mind-set. Advising must emphasize nonlinear, multifaceted, and open-ended forms of exploration that are most valued in the global economy of tomorrow.

Increasing numbers of students leave college without the necessary intellectual, social, and cultural capital to succeed in a global marketplace of ideas. Advisors play an important role by investing in this future. It is essential we continue the discussion of what it means to invest in a college education.

Action Steps

1. Investigate how your university finances amenities and extracurricular activities. Are the amenities that your school provides aligned with your values and long-term academic, career, and financial goals?
2. Write a vision for your life and post it somewhere you can see it every day. Each year this should be revisited for adjustment.
3. Review the *Occupational Outlook Handbook,* which provides useful information about various fields of study and encompasses projected percentage of job growth and the skills and educational background needed to work in that area.
4. Compare how much your college/university spends on initiatives that align directly with your values. If your number one priority for going to college is getting a job, how much does your college/university spend on job placement?

NOTES

1. Brian Jacob, Brian McCall, and Kevin M. Stange, "College as Country Club: Do Colleges Cater to Students' Preferences for Consumption?" Working Paper. *National Bureau of Economic Research*, January 2013. http://www.nber.org/papers/w18745.

2. G. D. Kuh, *High-impact Educational Practices: What They Are, Who Has Access to Them, and Why They Matter* (Washington, DC: Association of American Colleges and Universities, 2008).

3. Benjamin Ginsberg, *The Fall of the Faculty*. Reprint edition. (New York: Oxford University Press, 2013).

Chapter Four

Who Pays the Most for College?

At the Heart of Inequality

There is a student named Maria who wants to attend college. Her test scores are promising and she has done well in high school. This is particularly important since she attended an underperforming school in an urban school district. As a result of her hard work and following the advice of her guidance counselor, Maria received acceptance letters from two colleges in the mail: one from Somewhere University and another from Degreedy.

Maria knows that she will have to take out a loan to go to Somewhere University. If she chooses to attend Degreedy University, she will need even more assistance. Maria lives in a single-parent home and her mother cannot help her pay for tuition. Her mother never attended college and urges her to figure it out when she get there. Maria decides to talk it over with her guidance counselor.

After meeting with the counselor, Maria discovers that there are numerous ways to pay for college but that the majority of her college will be covered by unsubsidized Stafford student loans. Her mother refuses to help her with Parent PLUS loans because she has a bad credit history and is afraid that getting into the system will get her in more trouble. Maria fills out the FAFSA forms alone and hopes for the best. This feels more like a gamble than an investment.

Maria's mind shifts to a host of other concerns. If she majors in nursing, how much money will she make? Will she be able to buy a new car, a new home outside of her current neighborhood? Will she be able to help out her mother? What if she takes longer than four years to finish? How much more will that cost? How will she afford it?

She stares at a loan application for Somewhere University and wonders if she is mortgaging her life away. Will she be able to get a job after graduation that allows her to pay the student loans back? What will be her return on investment in comparison to that of her friends Jason, Heather, and Todd? How can she help her family if she will be paying back student loans for the next thirty years? Will attending college really improve her current situation?

Historically, a college degree has been seen as the quickest route to a better life in American society. The baccalaureate degree has historically been seen as the source of growth for the booming middle class and the golden ticket for those aspiring to join the American middle class. Although the middle class has struggled to keep its footing, the high regard for a college education has largely remained a constant fixation for most Americans.

For underrepresented communities, higher education meant much more—for some, it was being able to share newfound knowledge with family and friends, breaking barriers that lead to social change, being the first in the family to go to college, or having the experience of taking a class with a faculty member who resembled them or could relate to their background.

On the other side of this excitement for higher education was the ugly truth that, following graduation, underrepresented students would be underemployed and underpaid and would incur larger amounts of student loan debt than their counterparts. This chapter examines how student loans place an unequal burden on underrepresented populations and how discussions of college as an investment obscure the unequal dividends of a college education.

Maria's story is also a familiar one to thousands of families across the country. Since the 1990s, it has become increasingly difficult for students to finance college education but even more so for students from marginalized and underrepresented populations. In years past, the big question was whether underrepresented students would even attend college. While questions regarding opportunity and access remain a key concern today, as more qualified underrepresented students receive letters of acceptance from colleges across the country, the more pressing question is how will those that attend pay for it?

For example, in 1992–1993 the average student at most public colleges could expect to work part-time and cover most costs. Following the expansion of student financial aid with the GI Bill during the 1950s, there was an expectation that the federal subsidy of a college degree would contribute to both national priorities and economic vitality. This was not an entirely new concept during the 1950s, but students attending college were far less dependent on federal aid than in recent years.

Today nearly all students rely on some form of student aid in the form of federal and state aid grants and scholarships, but many are increasingly taking out loans. Despite the tremendous financial burden and risk that college presents for all students, black and Latino students are exposing themselves to far more risk than other students when they sign these promissory notes. This is somewhat paradoxical since federal support for higher education has increased and greater numbers of underrepresented students are attending college now than ever before.

However, as we discussed previously, the decision simply to attend college is no longer sufficient to address a variety of the complex and interlocking concerns of an increasingly competitive global marketplace. This is particularly true for students of color and other underrepresented groups that must be vigilant about the types of financial obligations they take on in college but also the types of colleges that they attend.

Studies have shown that Maria would be better off as a student and financially if she were matched with a school with similarly performing students and with similar financial needs. This type of decision requires understanding a variety of complex factors that are not readily available to students.

For example, most high school students are not sure which field of study will be beneficial to their professional interests and future. The fast pace of technology and increasing diversity of our population in the United States prompts students to change their careers up to nine times in their lifetime. Students like Maria need more access to college counseling and advising, but she is much more likely to attend a school where these services will be lacking.

Advising is multidimensional and it takes a village to assist with developing an effective but specialized personal and professional pathway toward a successful career and well-balanced life for students. In the case of underrepresented students, there are a few factors that work against their progress—lack of sociocultural capital, transformative assets, and inheritance; discrimination; stereotyping; and lack of mentorship.

Despite this reality many students enter college with ideas about cost and careers that are not aligned with the data. The rising cost of financing a college education combined with harsh realities of socioeconomic inequalities and uncertainties about the future labor market create conditions for disaster. In 2015, the *Debt Divide* report found that black and Latino students borrow more to obtain bachelor's degrees from both public and private institutions. Also, the report found that more blacks and Latinos drop out of college in debt without a college degree.[1]

Strategically maneuvering the roadblocks is possible; it just takes a little more focused energy and effort through communal support and leadership. Career discussions should begin earlier but not so early as to prevent students from developing curiosity and inquisitiveness, which is much more difficult to teach as they get older. Some countries like Germany have developed tracks for students seeking to pursue particular fields of study based on their demonstrated aptitude in high-stakes testing.

Considering the difficult racial legacy of inequality in the educational systems of the United States, it is unlikely that such a program could be fully adopted here. However, there are certainly bright spots to consider, such as investing more in vocational tracks during the high school years so that students who are gifted or evidence aptitude in such areas can be aware of other alternatives to the traditional four-year college plan.

As students change their careers at a rapid pace, they will also need to be the inventors of opportunities for others while creating change in a stagnant market. The waves of students born after 1980 are widely perceived as optimistic, socially engaged, and tech savvy. Their college cohort is the most diverse in American history and provides the creative fire and synergy to pursue new ventures that lead to the creation of new products and services for a global market.

Ironically, as the United States weathered the greatest economic downturn since the Great Depression, these students have been called lazy, unmotivated, and incompetent. Yet this generation, which matriculated in the era of corporatized colleges, has had to rely on the so-called American ethic of self-help more than any generation after World War II. Millennials seek out opportunities wide-reaching, expect feedback often, and are driven by their successes in their careers. The gap between the millennial and boomer generations has grown over the last several years in the workforce, so much so that communication between the two groups has become almost nonexistent.

THE MOST TO GAIN AND THE MOST TO LOSE: A MINORITY REPORT ON STUDENT LOANS

These factors are and will remain at the center of inequality facing underrepresented students in higher education because they cannot be eliminated using the analogy of the wise college investment. Students who stand to gain the most from college often have the most to lose. In an article in the *Chronicle of Higher Education* titled "Black Graduates Owe More Debt Than White, Asian, or Hispanic Graduates," the author Ashley Marchand found that in 2008 black students who attended private four-year or for-profit institutions borrowed more than they could afford to attend college.

In their 2010 study, authors Baum and Steele found that black students who earned a bachelor's degree accumulated an average debt of $30,500, whereas white students accrued $19,400. In 2011, total student debt had reached $1 trillion with compounded interest rates. While there are many lenders, including federal agencies, there have been some private organizations that have capitalized on the opportunity to cash in on the profits, such as Sallie Mae, Wells Fargo, Perkins, and Student Loan Express.

To make matters even worse, effective July 1, 2013, the student loan interest rate doubled, increasing the burden on young adults. Not only have market conditions driven the cost of higher education up, it has increased the burden on future leaders of America. In respect to access, not everyone has access to loans that provide a "reasonable" interest rate; in fact, a number of underrepresented students have not been able to reap the benefits of these kinds of loans. This creates a number of challenges for underrepresented and nontraditional students.

- First, the burden of debt serves as a lifetime sentence that renders them significantly disadvantaged in the financial marketplace. It decreases their likelihood of purchasing a home, traveling for family vacations, and investing in retirement.
- Second, the unemployment rate has historically been much higher for minorities, and once they do get a "job" they are underemployed and underpaid.
- Third, their growth at companies and firms often becomes stagnant because of a lack of a powerful network of mentors, sponsors, and supervisors who support their growth as professionals.

It has become a popular choice for American youth to take out student loans to pay for their education. The whole rationale behind this idea is to make a "down payment" on living the "American Dream" of success—new home, family, a white-collar job with health benefits and a 401k retirement plan. Has this ideology pushed students into having the perspective that they can purchase a degree and get an exorbitant return on their investment?

In reality, the whole philosophy of the "American Dream" provides a sense of falsehood for underrepresented students because in most cases, depending on their major, income earned does not outweigh the debt accrued. Derek Price (2012) has demonstrated, using data from wages and loan payments, how the financing of college education by loans is actually expanding the very socioeconomic gaps that higher education is supposed to address.

STUDENT BORROWERS BEWARE—ESPECIALLY IF THEY ARE UNDERREPRESENTED

Financial aid is a common way to finance your education. However, not everyone is eligible to receive it. It is based on the family's annual income. FAFSA is a federally funded initiative that provides students access to funding for college. Depending on which state students reside in they may be able to receive state and/or federally funded aid and access to subsidized or unsubsidized student loans. While these federally funded opportunities help subsidize the cost of education, there are hidden policies of which students and families should be aware. For example, Tuition Assistance Program (TAP) in New York State is limited to completing a specific number of credit hours toward one major. And once a student reaches the maximum credit hours for his/her major including general education requirements funding is discontinued.

Unsubsidized loans are given out more frequently but the interest rate is variable, which means that the cost of the loan can increase at any moment during the life of the loan. As a result, students can incur additional costs that are never recouped. A caveat that is common when students accept any type of loan is that if there is a credit at the end of the semester, most institutions issue a "refund" check. When students hear the word "refund" they automatically think that there is extra money left over. However, in actuality this money is a part of the loan that they will pay back to the lender with interest.

Taking loans to fund a student's college education may seem like the most logical way to get ahead and live the "American Dream." But it is not. There are a few reasons why this method is not feasible. First, the federal student loan debt has recently increased to $1 trillion, which means there are more students in debt and without employment. In addition to this, effective July 1, 2013, the student loan interest rate doubled, which has put more burden on young adults.

Second, it is generally assumed that upon a student's graduation they will start a business or find a job that will provide the income for a sustainable lifestyle. Students might want to save for a few years and then, perhaps, travel the world. Or they might want to prepare for starting a family, which means possibly buying a home, making some investments, and purchasing a reliable car. If students have an enormous amount of loan debt, it would become a burden on their financial stability.

Furthermore, underrepresented students are very susceptible to viewing college with a transactional mind-set because they have much more to lose. However, they lack the broader understanding of the cultural and nonlinear benefits of college and its role in the acculturation of the middle class. They are in a position to believe that the credential of college is the most important aspect of the process when educators, advisors, and alumni all understand that college is much more complex than choosing a profitable degree.

THE TRUE PRICE OF COLLEGE FOR UNDERREPRESENTED STUDENTS

Extending beyond the dollar amount, the true "price" of college is much higher for marginalized students who are balancing very complex demands on their resources, identity, and finances. Accounting for college we are really identifying three sacrifices: 1) sacrifice of scarce funds, 2) sacrifice of self, and 3) sacrifice of soul.

Sacrifice of scarce funds occurs when students are not able to afford college/university tuition and, if they are admitted to college, often work up to three jobs to make ends meet, taking the focus off intellectual development. Sharia, a Latina female and first-generation college student, decided to attend a small private institution to pursue a degree in forensic science. Part of her interest in the field stemmed from her desire to be a crime scene investigator.

One of Sharia's favorite shows, "Criminal Minds," kept her interest while in high school because of the complex murder cases they solved. Little did she know that there are very few of these types of positions available in the United States. Sharia received half of her tuition from scholarships but worked two jobs while attending college full-time. Her grades on average were in the B to C range. She eagerly invested her time, money, and commitment to the field, only to find out in her third year of college that she would not be employable in a field she loves.

Sacrifice of self occurs when students are giving up things that they think are most important about their intellectual abilities and interests to pursue degrees that are economically sensible or practical. Students focus on the outcome of obtaining a job after earning a college degree. As a result, they focus on a major that they do not enjoy or do well in for the pursuit of money. An example would be choosing a major that has more dollar potential instead of one that aligns with their strengths, passion, and purpose.

Sacrifice of soul occurs when marginalized students sacrifice the most because they are giving up a core of their collective cultural experiences to pursue degrees that are economically favorable in order to assimilate to American ideas. A large majority are focused on pursuing STEM fields, which typically include science-, technology-, engineering-, and mathematics-based disciplines. The average salaries in these fields is $65,000 and the job outlook is favorable. Underrepresented students in the STEM fields are given a complex and rigid curricular plan, exclusive of cultural experiences that strengthen and develop their cultural identity and self-efficacy. The solution is not to abandon these sacrifices but for students and colleges to work more closely on ways to share the burden of these experiences.

Furthermore, underrepresented students often feel pressured to demonstrate that they are above racial stereotypes. These tendencies and widespread public criticism of cultural awareness groups often prevent underrepresented students from participating in greater numbers in particular racial, cultural, and ethnic affinity groups. This has significant consequences because students are avoiding the types of college experiences that develop affinity groups central to their progression, retention, and graduation rates.

Students who miss out on these types of experiences are missing out on opportunities that have proven to have long-term impacts on their prospects in the workforce. For example, one study found participation in cultural groups to be significantly associated with numerous civic engagement and attitudes some six years after graduation.[2]

The question surrounding college funding becomes even more contentious as more states address the issues of undocumented students receiving in-state tuition. Many of these students were brought illegally to the United States by their parents and have grown up in an American context. Like many graduating students from high school, college ranks high on their list as being the ticket to the American Dream that brought their parents to the United States in the first place.

Many states have developed initiatives to assist these students in recognizing the important role they play in developing the local and regional economics of tomorrow. However, for many the process is frightening and threatening. They are pitted in a funds race against other students and families, and some states have even pursued funding that would prevent them from receiving the much needed in-state tuition help.

CREATIVE STRATEGIES FOR FINANCING COLLEGE

So, how does one finance their education? There are several ways to support a student's education without taking student or Parent PLUS loans, including but not limited to savings/investment, grants, scholarships, financial aid, and payment plans.

But in many of the cases students have to start their search for money early. This means parents will have to be engaged in their process at birth. Just think about it, if students invest $150 a month for seventeen years they will have a small nest egg to pay for their education. That's $30,600 without any interest accumulation or investment. Students could double this amount if they learn a little about the market.

While some students are unaware of this, there are some grants and scholarships available to supplement or provide a full ride for the first four years of college. It is wise to tread carefully when researching scholarship opportunities as there are hundreds of websites that are merely information-seeking scams. Students can begin their search with reputable organizations such as

Fastweb, Discus Awards, the Gates Millennium Scholars, Siemens Foundation, Holland & Knight Charitable Foundation, and the College Prowler.

Parents have also begun to make strategic moves to states that have strong support for higher education. For example, many parents have relocated to Georgia and become residents so that students can participate in the HOPE scholarship. Recently, New York State governor Andrew Cuomo announced free tuition for New York State residents. It can be done, a college education can be paid for in full, but it takes a concentrated amount of time and effort to research, organize, and apply to each individual opportunity.

Another way to go through college, even if you don't have a small nest egg, is to pay as you go. While it may not seem to be the most practical option, students will find that, in the end, it will work out for the best. Do you know why? Students will have no debt and will be free to prepare for the road ahead.

Many American students are realizing that they can save lots of money but gain impactful learning experiences by getting an education abroad. There are numerous American-based programs that allow students to study abroad and pick up college credit at a major discount compared to average tuition costs. In addition to these programs, some students elect to attend institutions abroad entirely.

CONCLUSION

In today's economy, many students are trying to figure out how they will finance their higher education. This is not an easy task, considering that the cost of a college education continues to soar. Students and parents from underrepresented demographics are rightfully asking, "Is college a good investment?" We argue that college is a good investment for underrepresented students but only if they are savvy about their choices and their finances.

Attending college is a milestone, but incurring college debt has become another kind of milestone for many students. It limits the future options and mobility that has brought many black and Latino/a students to college in the first place. All students, but especially these, should know how to build a portfolio that allows flexibility throughout their careers, meaning that students should be able to move seamlessly from one area to another.

More important, students will understand the importance of adopting the principle of becoming lifelong learners. This doesn't mean that students continue to return to college for education in a variety of areas but that they can develop their skill set as technology and trends change. Students can do this through reading books, attending seminars, and pursuing online education (e.g., Khan Academy, TedEx, MOOCs, etc.).

Action Steps

1. Find ways to pay for college through applying for scholarships and grants or building a small nest egg that supports your student's education starting as early as elementary school. This can be done with the assistance of school counselors and admissions advisors.
2. Invest in preparing students for college early by surrounding them with a diverse group of mentors, narrowing down the fields of interests, and developing an action plan that outlines feasible options for future careers.
3. Assist your student during middle and high school to develop a small startup business or project reflective of her or his interests that can assist with funding college.
4. Be aware of the road bumps that you may hit when working on a college track plan and help your student learn how to negotiate them.
5. Develop networks across racial, ethnic, and national boundaries. The role of informal networks will become more important in accessing opportunities during and following the college years.
6. What sacrifices will you have to make in order for your college investment to be worthwhile?

NOTES

1. Mark Huelsman. *The Debt Divide: The Racial and Class Bias Behind the "New Normal" of Student Borrowing* (New York: Demos, 2018).
2. Bowman et al. (2014) "Student Involvement in Ethnic Student Organizations: Examining Civic Outcomes Six Years After Graduation," *Research in Higher Education*, vol. 56, no. 2 (March 2015): 127–45.

Chapter Five

What Is Your College Education Worth?

The Dangers of Investment Mentalities and Jargon on Higher Learning

Aimee is no stranger to college. Her mother was overjoyed when she received the letter of acceptance to Somewhere University. However, after she reviews the price for one year at Somewhere University she is taken aback. "There is no way that we can afford this!" she tells Aimee. "There is no way that one year of college is worth that!" When Aimee's father sees the cost, he agrees. "No degree is worth that much, particularly your degree in Communications. I have seen so many of my friends' children working at coffee shops and delivering packages. You would be better off working now than paying all of that money for nothing!"

Aimee wonders to herself whether her parents are right. After just four years at Somewhere University, she will have accumulated more than $36,000 in student debt. She knows that she can expect to earn around $50,000 a year if she is lucky to find a job. For Aimee, the question is not if her degree will pay off but when and how much. Her parents are less patient. They need her to help take care of her ailing grandmother, and college isn't paying anything anytime soon.

Aimee talks with a recent graduate from Somewhere University in her program of interest. Michael graduated a few years prior and was not doing well. He had taken out loans like she planned to do but had not found a job. "I had hoped to have a house of my own now but I still live with my parents and most of my check goes to paying back my loans," Michael remarked.

Aimee grew more discouraged. She saw dozens of postings for new jobs in her field but they all required work experience in addition to a bachelor's degree. How could she afford not to attend college? Wasn't going to college supposed to automatically qualify her for these positions and help her make more money? More specifically, how could she get these experiences and afford to pay for her college education? Maybe her parents were right after all.

Aimee's story is a familiar one to thousands of families across the country. Students know how to work hard at jobs to make ends meet but fail to apply that same hustle ethic to the classroom. As a result, they passively expect college to accomplish what they can only bring about through persistence and high levels of engagement. If students and parents expect college to pay off, they need to act like it. They must view college like the risk that it is.

Even for students who are not the first in their family to attend college, the sticker price for colleges is getting them to question the worth of college. Since the late 1990s, tuition and fees at public institutions have skyrocketed as states have scaled back their support for public education. Many private institutions have faced similar challenges at keeping the sticker price of college accessible to their targeted student populations. The increase in the cost of college has significantly impacted the majors that students pursue while enrolled.

Gone are the days when students perused the course catalog to explore the horizons of an unfamiliar field for curiosity's sake. Students and parents nervously watch the "clock" while the tuition bill rapidly accrues. Facing mounting financial burdens of tuition and uncertain prospects in the wage and labor market, many students hedge their bets on what they perceive to be safe, "profitable" degrees.

Numerous web stories posted by PayScale and *Forbes* clickbait readers into salivating over a future with a "profitable" major. These commercials for the corporatization of higher education further imply that the worth of college should be defined by the immediate postgraduate value of a particular degree in the marketplace. Parents and students increasingly use the terms "pragmatic" and "profitable" interchangeably. They assume that because a degree in English or Art History does not often entail a corporate mailing address with a signing bonus that these areas of study are largely irrelevant. These shortsighted views not only shortchange the college experience for thousands of students but also sacrifice the very skills that they need to pursue the economic value they so desire.

Many students may be allowing sticker shock and a few short-sighted interpretations of financial worth to narrowly determine their understanding of the purpose of college and the broader economic possibilities of higher education. Despite rising costs, college remains a sound financial decision but only when students realize that the true worth is not in the degree. Very few students are comparing their options and seeking alternatives to the current arrangement.

There are numerous ways that students can achieve diverse economic goals by pursuing less traditional paths to a college education. They need to take advantage of a variety of innovative arrangements by some of the more creative institutions emerging in the higher educational marketplace.

- Apprenticeship training programs that prepare students to work in the contracting industry (e.g., electrician, plumbing, wood working, etc.)
- Business incubator certificates that pair students up with mentors who guide them to build start-ups
- Educational coaching and targeted skill development exercises and assessments
- Free online courses that teach critical thinking, writing, and problem solving skills

In the last twenty years, a disproportionate amount of attention has been placed upon the degree itself as if it were a piece of paper granting magical worth to those who were able to endure years of privation, indoctrination, and torture. The way that students talk of graduation throughout their college years is almost exclusively focused on the paper and not the experience itself. Some students balk at the amount of reading and assignments. Many dare ask a question that would have been taboo just a generation ago, "Do I have to buy this book?"

Louis Menand's essay "Live and Learn" exposes the fundamental differences that an emerging generation whose college experiences have been framed largely in a transactional mind-set presents. The rise of standardized testing in elementary and secondary education coupled with the increasing role of the learning outcomes movement are partially to blame as they have shifted the culture of learning from being spontaneous and multivariate to linear and predetermined.[1]

Consequently, we have now seen two generations that understand college as having value only as a place where they receive grades and diplomas but otherwise as a distraction to future plans and ambitions. The slow, reflective, and transformational aspects of collegiate study have been increasingly replaced by fast-paced, checklist-oriented educational models that promise more but deliver less.

These experiences and the way that increasing numbers of students have innovated upon their own purpose for enrolling in higher education undermines some of the most important aspects of the college experience: curiosity, creativity, innovation, and engagement. The experience of college is where the real worth is, and the value of that experience is very difficult to quantify in ways that are meaningful to everyone. This is an unfortunate trend that is another example of how equating college as purely a financial decision not only fundamentally distorts the worth of higher education but also inevitably causes economic harm to those who pursue such strategies.

THE WORTH OF SKILLS IN THE KNOWLEDGE ECONOMY

A core reason that thinking about college as an investment is harmful is that having a limited understanding of the marketplace makes students unprepared for what they should focus on while in college. Students today no longer compete for jobs locally but rather globally. Education and technical training should be based not only on the American economy but also trends in the world.

Students and their parents often have tunnel vision because, unless they take personal initiative, the existing educational system exposes them to little information about the competitive realities of the global marketplace. The existing assessment regime in secondary education is designed largely to assess what is easily captured and profitably marketed by large-scale testing companies, educational policymakers, and besieged educational administrators. This experience sets students up for failure in college.

The deep types of learning, interpersonal skills, work ethic, and intellectual curiosity that students need to prosper in a global economy are not easily measured in this existing arrangement. These skills require deep reflection, grow slowly, and will present some unwelcome truths about the status quo that neither parents nor students have been willing to accept. Consequently, students and their parents fall back on an old myth that as long as they invest in the process of education itself inevitably their lives will be improved substantially. There is a ring of truth to this but as it relates to economic fortunes this is a myth that must be debunked.

There are particular paths of study that develop the types of transferable skills to make one competitive in the marketplace. These include critical thinking, mathematical thinking, and creative thinking. These types of skills are not easily developed— in other words it is very difficult to take a one-month workshop and learn how to be a critical thinker. These skills take years of development and practice but yield very important transferable abilities that augment nearly everything else that a person chooses to do.

When students approach college attempting to avoid development of these very significant but important skills it hurts their abilities to perform in other areas that the marketplace may be placing a high demand on. So a student who wants to focus exclusively on programming but thinks that art history or literature is completely irrelevant is likely not to thrive in either. Perhaps more important, students who don't develop critical thinking, reading, and writing skills tend never to do so over the development of their career, and the market punishes them for that whether they are college graduates or not.

Following the publication of *Academically Adrift*, many colleges came under fire for not delivering on the promises they made. The report found that students are studying less than ever while earning higher grades. The book listed a series of majors that are notorious for producing students fit for the marketplace but unfit for higher educational outcomes. The authors concisely argued that there was very little learning taking place on college campuses and that employers were beginning to notice the declining quality of graduates.

The investment mentality regarding higher education is certainly one factor that contributed to this dilemma. When students and parents began to see college as a consumer product rather than a culturally and economically unique institution, they misinterpreted what the actual product was that they were buying. Too often they see themselves as buying an assured outcome rather than an honest evaluation. When the consumers of college are more interested in the credential than the assessment this outcome is inevitable. Colleges delivered the degrees and grades that parents and students demanded while professors chafed under the egregious changes and employers winced at the product: high achieving graduates lacking fundamental skills and initiative.

These students perceive themselves as gifted with their degrees but in actuality that credential is only as good as the skills they have gained. The degree provides the shorthand for potential employers and certifies that students are capable of the work but it is the actual skills that employers will increasingly become attracted to instead of the imprimatur of a college education. This is particularly true for the majority of students who will not attend the world's twenty-five most prestigious institutions.

The vast majority of students will have to prove themselves in a marketplace that is so specialized in the competency of key skills that the degree will play an increasingly diminished role. This is not to say that a degree is worthless because it is not. Perhaps in the last forty to fifty years there has been an overreliance on thinking of the college degree as a credential separate from any particular skills that the bearer of that degree may possess.

Furthermore, in the global knowledge-based economy, the benefits of an education do not always provide an immediate return on investment. Additionally, the economic returns are often non-linear. In other words, there are few investments that people can make that guarantee a predictable rate of return. The instruments that provide the most reliable returns are often so small that one can end up losing money in the process. For example, a savings account is an excellent place to stash cash but it is one of the worst places to keep one's money safe from inflation. The interest rates that one can expect from a bank are incredibly small and insignificant. However, this small return on investment is a risk that many are willing to take because they cannot stomach greater risks.

This same type of mentality can be applied to the college education. A college degree in itself is a safe bet to place one's money upon but increasingly the rate of returns is smaller and smaller in comparison to what one pays for the degree. The value of the degree itself is also worthy of risk assessment. This is especially true depending on the type of major one studies. A degree of any kind does not guarantee a return.

There have been numerous examples of individuals expecting that a high-performing degree today would continue to do the same indefinitely. Historically this has not been the case. Graduates with high-performing degrees in computer science and engineering during the Great Recession also faced the same challenges as those in less technical fields. Some may view a college education as a speculative investment since certain degrees that are worth a lot in the marketplace today can be worth less tomorrow.

However, if students are truly engaged in the types of learning that college provides, a degree may be worth *less* today than it was yesterday, but if that student had been truly educated the degree is not worthless. When we shift the focus from the credential to the experiences, we find that the skills that a student may attain can be readily reconstituted and redeployed in other areas that may not have been assessable prior to education. That is where the true value lies!

For example, initial assessments on the long-term viability of the humanities major can be misleading because it has never been about the credential—it's about the skills! Students majoring in degrees like English, history, arts, and religion are often told that these degrees are a waste of time and money (or "not worth the paper they are printed on," according to one financial expert).

However, multiple studies have shown that this conventional wisdom is quite misleading. Students who major in the humanities and other related fields often graduate making less money than many of the other more market-driven job-specific majors such as business, accounting, and marketing. Despite this initial gap, studies have shown that over the duration of a career these majors do quite well financially, in some cases outperforming those with professional degrees.[2]

When the faddishness of the degree fades away, what remains are the *core skills,* relationships, and experiences that one has collected. These core competencies will allow one to retool and work in another field or have the mind-set to be reeducated in another line of work. These core skills are valuable to economic growth, but are they worth the money that students and governments invest with expectations for a promise of economic growth? The answer is complicated, but, increasingly, skeptics are responding—no.

Alison Wolf's *Does Education Matter?* offers one of the earlier takes on this question. Writing broadly to address the educational landscape in the United Kingdom, Wolf argues that there is little economic benefit to spending more on higher education in order to stimulate growth. However, her argument is not anti-education. She merely urges readers to assess whether the increased commitment of resources to higher education has resulted in outcomes desired and whether those funds may be better allocated elsewhere in the educational supply chain.

When people talk of the knowledge-based economy, they are really talking about skills. Thinking more carefully about the relationship between knowledge versus skills has historically been less of an area of emphasis in college, with some notable exceptions. Skills are important, but the kinds of knowledge that a student experiences in the close, confined, concentrated environs of college in certain disciplines are very difficult, though not impossible, for students to replicate elsewhere.

Learning to code is an important form of literacy for the future; however, the kinds of skills coding promises are very narrow and specific to that domain. In order for students to appreciate this skill, they often have to approach it from a collected background in other areas. Some disciplines appear better equipped to address the development of certain "marketable" skills than others.

The knowledge economy is the creative economy, and it is more difficult for students to become creative enough to reinvent and retool themselves when they lack initiation into some of the most fundamental areas that have sustained human intellect for thousands of years. When students completely substitute commercial training for the broader but more slowly developed abilities in critical reading, writing, art, music, and other areas it results in a more one-dimensional rendering of learning, which hurts both students and college and universities.

WHEN THE COLLEGE EXPERIENCE IS WORTH LESS

Over the last several years, there have been major changes in the higher education landscape. Marketing has led many students to believe that to get a degree means to get a good job with a salary, but it is more than that. It's about developing a portfolio of experiences that highlight their individual and collective strengths. When we think of college as an investment, we have to examine the college experience as a whole. Holistic discovery of self through experiential learning and education is sidelined in the process.

College is becoming more expensive and more important, but increasing numbers of students do not know what college is about and how to make the best of their experiences. It is essential that students think about their college experience in a holistic form that challenges them for a lifetime and teaches them to think competitively and collaboratively, especially with the demands of today's competitive global marketplace. There are four essential skills that students need to develop in college:

1. Curiosity/exploration
2. Critical thinking and questioning
3. Creativity and originality
4. Purpose and identity

Instead of taking students through a linear process, in which they master each skill in one year, it is important we effectively advise students to develop throughout their experience.

Making the most of one's experience involves capitalizing on opportunities that have been laid in the foundation of college education, such as internships, serving as a teaching assistant, career services (resume writing, mock interviews, etc.), alternative spring breaks, study abroad, being mentored by faculty, poster/research presentations, coordinating events, serving in a leadership capacity through living and learning communities, writing workshops, entrepreneur hubs, and much more. It's not simply about going through the motions but being intentional with actions that will bring results while they are in college.

The more students engage in activities, the more they learn about their likes and dislikes. James, a criminal justice major at a small private Catholic institution, was in his sophomore year and was thinking about pursuing a career in law. He participated in a summer law institute for undergraduate students at a large public university. It was a residential program that gave students a glimpse into the field of law. They conducted mock trials, studied prevalent cases, prepped for the LSAT exam, and connected with other students with similar interests. For James, participating in this program was a deciding factor that led him to not attend law school.

APPLES TO ORANGES: INVESTING IN DEEP LEARNING AND RELATIONSHIPS INSTEAD OF GRADES AND CREDENTIALS

Over the last several years, there has been a national call at American universities to change the tide of the educational system. Many institutions are beginning to understand the importance of applied learning and are introducing experiential learning opportunities. These are activities that augment students' experiences outside of the classroom, such as community service, internships, study abroad, and alternative spring break trips. The purpose is to engage students with hands-on activities that encourage them to think more critically and eventually lead to the invention of products, services, and goods.

bell hooks' classic book *Teaching to Transgress,* which stresses the importance of teaching as performative act that challenges students to become more engaged outside of the classroom setting, still applies, even though it was written several years ago. Education is more than a transaction, it is a foundation meant to launch students into a bigger world where they can explore their passion and soar to their potential.

Another reason that thinking about college as an investment is harmful is because students are comparing apples to oranges. College is an expensive endeavor and undoubtedly it should be taken seriously. Every dollar should be taken into account. However, the increasing overreliance on financial jargon to describe one of the most important educational experiences in the modern era severely distorts the nature of the transaction that is under way. If there is one mantra in the financial world that everyone has heard it is "diversify."

By that, financial advisors mean to differentiate the types of investments one places their money in based upon one's particular financial goal. So, for example, there is a tendency to recommend supposedly less volatile investments like bonds over riskier investments in stocks; but further yet, even within the stock market, individuals must decide what sectors to invest in because some are inherently riskier than others. The technology sector is notorious for being a highly volatile industry, and buyers of equities in this sector are consistently warned that a very small number of these start-ups go on to become large-scale profitable companies.

Ironically, some students are being counseled to invest thousands of dollars of borrowed money, essentially borrowing on margin, to pursue degrees in one of the most volatile sectors of the global economy. We would never counsel students to max several credit cards out to invest in equities, yet every year we encourage thousands of students to sign away their economic futures by pushing them to pursue careers in STEM fields without regard for the inherent risk that involves.

Arguably, STEM education and careers are important and will probably continue to be for quite some time. However, when students are corralled into these majors without adequately assessing these risks, student aptitude, and a more holistic picture of what's taking place in higher education becomes misleading.

Popular discussions about student loan-to-debt ratios are worthwhile but can be misleading for several reasons. If it is true that we view college as an investment, then why is there an expectation to see an immediate return on investment in the years following graduation? If the same logic is applied similarly to financial investments, the inconsistencies become more apparent. What financial advisor would advocate making a $100,000 investment and expecting a 100 percent return within four years? Historically, we know that despite the turbulence that exists yearly in the marketplace, the return on invested capital across the long term teaches us that a carefully planned portfolio is the best investment that one can make with their money.

Another way to think about it is this. In 1997 a book was published entitled *Die Broke*. The author suggested that it was better for retirees to spend their money while they were alive and enjoy their money living "rich" than to die living the life of a pauper in a large estate. The fundamental argument of this book was that if people invested their wealth during their prime years to causes and people that they wanted, they could live much more meaningful lives and see the fruit of their investment.

Paradoxically, many students attending colleges and universities today are espousing such an approach by signing away future earnings to live a moderately luxurious life, pursuing careers based on assumptions of future returns rather than aptitude or passion. This is complicated further by the fact that they are living at a standard that for many will be difficult to replicate once they are in the workforce.

In the past there was a saying "living like a student" used euphemistically for people who were living so miserly that they were saving money. Today in many colleges and universities, this is not the case. The student housing industry is now a billion-dollar enterprise as dozens of private firms flood the university market to provide students with luxury-style amenities.

In 2010, Peter Thiel launched an investment experiment called the Thiel Fellowship that made headlines by promising prospective college graduates that he would make them an offer they couldn't refuse. If students would forgo the formality of the four-year rite of passage and delve directly into entrepreneurship, Thiel promised his foundation would back them. The first class was quite impressive, including a roster of students of diverse talents and backgrounds. When the experiment drew to an end in 2013, the results made several things clear.[3]

Thiel's investment in the students had paid off but not in the ways that many people expect of college education. The parameters for the success of Thiel's student were based on if they were doing as well or were better off financially than their counterparts in college. This comparison is an important analysis but an unfair comparison for several reasons.

Thiel's focus assumes that if a student had $100,000 and a choice to invest that money in college or entrepreneurship, the student would be better off pursuing learning in the real world. What Thiel's experiment showed is not that students are better off going to college but that having access to start-up capital and elite networks plays a disproportionate role in a student's overall trajectory of success.

Nevertheless, the comparison is an important one since the stupefying levels of student debt prevent students from taking the same types of ventures immediately after graduation in the years that they would be most beneficial. As for Thiel's class, many of them had developed productive companies of their own and had certainly made good on the investment of dollars in entrepreneurship that in Thiel's opinion would've been squandered on the vagaries of college mediocrity.

Thiel's investment in entrepreneurship teaches us several things about the worth of the college experience. It goes without saying that relationships matter and if students are not developing these important kinds of mentoring relationships with faculty, staff, industry experts, community partners, and other students then they are squandering missed opportunity.

Thiel's students were successful not only because of the initial money that he invested in them but also because of his association with them. They gained access to his network, his prestige, and his support systems. These types of relationships are at the core of what makes college a valuable social experience.

Without abusing the limitations of this analogy, college graduates should also think about the long-term benefits of their investment. Teaching students to "place all bets" in fads in the marketplace for majors where there is high demand but failing to develop the time-tested skills proven over centuries of academic life is irresponsible. Conversely, students choosing to major in fields without doing ample research on how this knowledge may be applied upon graduation is equally irresponsible. What students need now, more than ever before, is to invest in a diversity of learning outcomes.

It is very difficult to monetize college as an investment because the value of relationships, networks, knowledge, and experimental exploration are very difficult to quantify but are at the center of the worth of college. Thomas Alva Edison's successful improvisation on the incandescent light filament is an example showing that having the ability and space to learn and innovate are financially important steps to commercial viability. Contemporary society fawns over the latest technological entrepreneurs but seldom celebrates the institutions, structures, and culture of learning that have so often contributed to such important commercial successes.

So how does one learn to invest in the relationships and the full potential of learning so integral to holistic college experiences rather than merely focusing on the raw economic potential of college credentials? Is it possible to be fully invested in acquiring financially feasible degrees while simultaneously developing the more intrinsic aspects of self-discovery and meta learning? As one might expect, the answer is complicated.

As long as college is perceived primarily as an avenue to make more money, the vast majority of students will never realize the most important aspects of higher education. As students see college degrees as a commodity, to be bought and traded with dispatch in anticipation of a monetary reward, colleges and universities will continue to suffer and ironically be significantly hindered in bestowing the economic advantages so many have come to expect.

THE MARKET REWARDS RISK, NOT CONFORMITY

Another troubling but equally important part of this debate that is being left out is that there are some valuable things that college provides that are contrary to market values. Often these insights are rewarded economically but sometimes they provide a deep sense of satisfaction that has not always been captured in economic measurement. College perhaps is the last great public institution in which every measurement of transformation is not directly tied to profit.

For many, it is threatening to have such a ubiquitous institution whose sole purpose is not reinforcing the economic status quo. By no means does this excuse much of the waste that takes place on college campuses or many of the structural problems that have been presented by critics of the current model. These points should, however, urge us to more carefully consider the values that a college experience enshrines and how to make that a possibility for every student who desires it.

College is very much valued as a place to take controlled risks and to receive valuable feedback from a variety of experts. Most students have been indoctrinated to think that less feedback is better. When many students receive a graded essay and see that the paper has been mortally wounded by a red pen, comments sprawling across the margins, there is a certain primal instinct to panic.

Many professors will attest that the vast majority of students do not read the comments but simply go to the grade. The ones who do read the comments often view them as an affront or sometimes a textual assault on their intellectual abilities. Those comments, more so than the grade, are one of the most valuable artifacts of college life.

The same professor who so willingly offers up office hours to students and copious commentary on papers will charge thousands of dollars in consulting fees if requested for similar services off campus. The efficiencies of scale in the college classroom allow students to receive such individualized attention at a relative bargain, yet so few students take advantage of the available expertise.

One of the most important lessons that students can learn in college is all of the alternative ways to use college to achieve the financial goals they seek. However, if one has financial goals to launch the next Fortune 500 company or technology giant, it is safe to say that one has to be willing to take risks that the majority of other people are not taking. There is an apocryphal assumption that to take these risks students need to divest from college, but they need to do exactly the opposite.

Students need to invest much more deeply in the types of collegiate experiences that will provide them with the competitive edge to compete in the global marketplace. This edge is gained not by switching majors to the next fad but rather taking an honest assessment of one's intellectual curiosity, aptitude, and abilities to align them with opportunities that ensure the desired outcomes.

CONCLUSION

College advisors and parents often talk about a college degree as an investment, but college will only pay off when students are engaged in the kinds of experiences that are intellectually challenging and personally meaningful and that teach them to be economically competitive. In recent years, far too much attention has been focused on the economic worth of a college education in isolation. Students, parents, and educators have forgotten that college is valuable only when it connects to a meaningful personal and intellectual mission.

While the cost of college remains a concern, motives to save money and to make good on an expensive "investment" must not overshadow the true purpose of higher education. By pursuing and proactively creating experiences that emphasize in-depth learning and engage the full range of curiosity in their learning, more students are realizing that the worth of a college education is not the credential itself. Saving money and pursuing less traditional paths to a college education abroad is perhaps one of the most valuable forms of education that students can pursue.

Critiques of the economic viability of college couched solely in investment jargon lack the language to describe worth in other ways. These descriptions narrow our perception of the possibility of higher education and the purpose of learning. Despite rising costs, college remains a sound financial decision but only when students realize that the worth is not in the paper but in the ability to take controlled risks and leverage the networks of knowledge.

It is likely that if Aimee bases her educational decisions purely on the ability to earn more working today than in the near future with a college degree of any major, she will most likely see her earnings significantly decrease over the course of her lifetime. Aimee may want to reconsider the worth of a college education outside of the limited perspectives of an economic investment. There are a surprising number of alternative approaches to a college education that bring back those elements of higher education worth investing in.

Action Steps

1. Focus on the development of specific skills instead of grades.
2. Encourage students to test out their ideas and areas of strengths through the creation of a small business.
3. Evaluate the costs of a variety of educational opportunities: community college, four-year university, and trade schools.
4. Develop up to four different ways your student can obtain technical training or education through the college or university without taking out student loan debt. For example, fund community college out of pocket and have your student focus on a specialized technical skill. Allow the student to work for a few years and go back to obtain their college degree.
5. Enroll your student in at least one professional and personal development opportunity per year outside of work and school activities. This will allow time for reflection on his/her purpose, identity, and future goals. Ask them the key question: What problem do they want to solve?

NOTES

1. Michael Bennett and Jacqueline Brady, "A Radical Critique of the Learning Outcomes Assessment Movement," *The Radical Teacher*, no. 94 (Fall 2012): 34–47.

2. George Anders, "Good News Liberal Arts Majors: Your Peers Probably Won't Outearn You Forever," Wall Street Journal, September 12, 2016; Robert N. Charette (2013). "Is It Fair to Steer Students into STEM Disciplines Facing a Glut of Workers?" *IEEE Spectrum*. https://spectrum.ieee.org/riskfactor/at-work/tech-careers/stem-crisis-as-myth-gets-yet-another-workout; "Hunting for Soft Skills, Companies Scoop Up English Majors," accessed October 31, 2016, http://finance.yahoo.com/news/hunting-soft-skills-companies-scoop-140100691.html; Yi Xue and Richard Larson, "STEM Crisis or STEM Surplus? Yes and Yes," Monthly Labor Review, U.S. Bureau of Labor Statistics, May 2015, https://doi.org/10.21916/mlr.2015.14.

3. Catherine Clifford, "These Kids Just Got $100,000 to Drop out of School," Entrepeneur, June 5, 2014; Tom Clynes, "Peter Thiel's Dropout Army," *The New York Times*, June 4, 2016. http://www.nytimes.com/2016/06/05/opinion/sunday/peter-thiels-dropout-army.html.

Chapter Six

Why Is It Important to Invest in Yourself?

Success Strategies for When the College Bubble Bursts

Ashley has always dreamed of attending college. Her test scores are average and she has done well in high school. One of the best words of advice Ashley received from her high school guidance counselor was to "Stay curious and ask questions!" She was encouraged to feed her personal interests instead of learning the minimum to pass a particular class or just cramming for the test.

Early on Ashley learned to balance the need to get good grades with her personal passion for learning and problem solving. She learned that good grades do not necessarily correspond with learning. One of the key characteristics that set Ashley aside from her classmates was her curiosity. She was able to find something that interested her in every topic discussed in class. This characteristic did not come naturally but through years of practice and a willingness to ask questions.

Whenever Ashley was faced with a subject that she didn't understand or like, she always found something about the topic that interested her and began to raise questions. As a result, Ashley developed the invaluable skill of posing critical and creative questions. She has learned how to search for new answers beyond what her teachers expected of her. This self-directed attitude toward learning set her apart from most of her peers in high school.

The same steadiness of curiosity followed Ashley to college. While Ashley's friends rushed off to major in science and technology fields and to choose colleges based on what they thought that the job market would return, Ashley made her selection based on other criteria. She asked different questions about the flexibility of the curriculum, student-to-professor ratios, part-

time to full-time faculty ratios, availability of support staff, administrative to faculty overhead, and student governance to determine which college was the right fit for her.

At the heart of her college search, Ashley sought to address one fundamental question: How does this college address my diverse interests and needs through its curriculum and experiences while providing me a solid return on what I am paying? She was not content or distracted with the promises of the admissions office and the hype of the facilities. Ashley asked herself how this college would help her develop into the type of person she wanted to become and whether it would be worth it.

Ashley's story is a familiar one to thousands of families across the country. Since the 2000s, the costs of colleges and universities have increased at a rate that has pushed increasing amounts of debt on students. The wages that students expect upon graduation often do not meet the minimum needs for a middle class.

Following the rapid expansion of student debt, there was an expectation that wages would increase, but that has not been the case in most fields. Even in high-demand areas, students must face fierce competition from global competitors who are nimbler, due to significant structural investments in higher education that the United States can no longer compete with.

Expansion from local to global competition has sent even more students to college with expectations that more advanced degrees will provide a competitive advantage, but this has not been the case. Instead, this has created a higher demand for what has further contributed to the rising costs of higher education—a bubble. When the college bubble bursts, students will need more than a credential—yes, they'll need a college degree but will have to demonstrate what they have learned in college and how to effectively play the game with real-world competition on the fly.

Although it is important for students to graduate from college, this should not be the ultimate goal of the college experience. As Bennett and other college critics have pointed out, numerous graduates such as Bill Gates, Russell Simmons, Peter Thiel, Sean Combs, Mark Zuckerberg, and others never graduated from college but went on to live productive lives. Instead of using these individuals as a point to undermine the relevance of college, we think it is particularly important to examine what these individuals were doing while they were in college to enrich the experience for other students.

While Bennett and Thiel's views on college have many evangelists in the current economic climate, the conventional wisdom and economic data still support college as a wise choice. Ironically, many of the paragons of the anti-college trends are vocal supporters of the college experience and urge youth not to follow the path that led them to drop out of college. College is not a perfect place, but it provides a useful platform for success, if the proper strategies are employed.

HACKING COLLEGE

Perhaps the most important question that we should be asking here is, if Gates, Thiel, and Zuckerberg had never attended college at all, would they have been introduced to the core ideas that they used to make themselves successful? Would they have developed a network of friends and knowledge that allowed them to expand their ideas? Would they have been given opportunities to test their ideas before applying them in the real world?

Students who are effectively able to engage these questions while in college are much more able to realize its worth and potential to transform their lives. Focusing exclusively on graduation rates minimizes the significance of independent lines of inquiry that are developed during college that have no point of completion. It is the nurturing and development of curiosity that is a key strength of the college experience. However, it is precisely these types of experiences that are difficult to measure and thus are rarely included in critiques of higher education.

Steve Jobs taught us that our strategy in college should be about the quest for creativity and the perfection of ideas. Known for his extraordinary invention of the iPhone, Steve Jobs showed us that innovation of technology is key to successful growth and global connections. The iPhone is a household name internationally, and it all started with an idea and a plan.

Bill Gates teaches us that our strategy in college should focus on identifying academic mentoring and advising to help us properly sequence learning and coursework so that it yields the most benefit. Gates has corrected as inaccurate those who characterize him as a college dropout. He affirms that he attended college and completed enough credit hours but never fulfilled enough courses to graduate in any major. In part, this has led Gates to crusade for efforts to maximize graduation rates and to also counsel those seeking to emulate him to stay in college.

Mark Zuckerberg teaches us that our strategy in college should be to fine-tune and test entrepreneurial ideas. The storied rise of Facebook is a textbook case of personal ambition, but it is also an important parable about how to make good ideas better. Zuckerberg illustrates that the purpose of college is not merely to prepare to work for someone else but to develop and build on one's own ideas and to test them out until one arrives at an acceptable (or profitable) conclusion.

Ted Turner teaches us that our strategy in college is to challenge conventions and unsettle accepted norms. Before Turner became the magnate of cable television he was studying economics in college and was kicked out for having a coed in his dormitory room (then against campus policy). No one should go to college expecting to become rich. What makes students prosper is their ability to be innovative with learning experiences.

Risk takers like Turner, Gates, and Thiel are exceptions to the rule and deviate from the norm. The extremes of wealth come from a variety of luck, hard work, connections, intelligence, and risk. The right combination of these factors proved to make Turner a very wealthy man, but the proportions of these behaviors can also set one up for failure in college. Many college dropout success stories are square pegs trying to fit in a circle hole. They tend to be fairly well-adjusted people who are like everyone else but they have certain ideas or passions that prevent them from following the well-trodden path.

Peter Thiel teaches us that our strategy in college should be to challenge economic inequality. Thiel is often cited as being a college dropout although he earned three degrees. He has three claims to fame: founding PayPal, having an outsized political profile, and paying students $100,000 to drop out of college and pursue entrepreneurship instead. The initial successes from his dropout academy have revealed a disturbing theme: for those students who have initiative, drive, and intelligence, entrepreneurship without college in the short term can be a preferable path if you are rich.

Thiel's experiment is much more a critique of the role of economic inequality in our society than the utility of college. It hints that college is not the meritocratic economic sorting bin that many perceive it to be; we live in a society where the initial access to wealth is often more important than the accoutrements of higher education.

PLANNING FOR THE POST–HIGHER ED BUBBLE BURST

Another key strategy to properly invest for college success is to plan for the unforeseeable, not the fad. When the college bubble burst does happen, it will be much more meaningful to demonstrate what one has learned and examples of application in real-world scenarios. This does not mean that one should only pursue a course that focuses on the application of knowledge—it's quite the contrary. Students should explore a variety of esoteric and creative pursuits while using college as a laboratory to explore their own combinations of these ideas.

One thing that all the college dropouts above share in common is that they were in pursuit of an elusive idea or goal that had not yet materialized. They did not see the credential college provided as the end goal, but rather they viewed college experiences and achievements as tools to help them on the way. Far too many students today plan their majors around fads instead of trends that they are intellectually passionate about and emotionally invested in.

Helping students plan their academic major and career can be a life changing process. It is essential that students choose a major that complements their strengths, interests, and creativity. With an unstable economy, mapping out a four-year plan for college and, more specifically, career is more crucial than ever.

Many students who graduate with a bachelor's degree end up working two or three part-time jobs outside of their field to make ends meet. There are a few reasons for this: lack of retirement of older employees, fewer opportunities available in the fields of humanities and social sciences, and the lack of critical thinking skills of new graduates.

The authors of the famous book *Academically Adrift: Limited Learning on College Campuses* believe that college education has become watered down and does not offer the necessary practical skills for success in American society and globally. The lack of academic rigor is the cause of failure of college graduates, and the authors believe that there should be a shift from "social engagement" to strictly "academic engagement."

While this is a valid point, we believe that a holistic focus on the entire learning process works best in teaching students—that is, not focusing only on academics but also survival skills in this new age economy, where one does not stay in one place of employment for thirty years. The fact of the matter is that students must be prepared for jobs that are not currently in existence. This kind of work has all but dissipated and what is left for our beloved student is the rough exterior of a world that has billions of people who have a variety of skills competing for work. The lack of employment is not the only thing under fire, but the type of degree one earns as well.

Recently, higher education news reports have bombarded the media airways, chanting "liberal and social science degrees are worthless" as they don't provide students with a solid career for the future; it's suggested that what's better are the hard-core sciences, math, and engineering. Most especially, PhD holders in these fields (i.e., liberal arts and social sciences) have been intensely criticized. Lack of preparation to enter a field that has a variety of options, terrible career advisement, and decrease of teaching opportunities in the fields of liberal arts and social sciences have been blamed.

Students most affected in these majors are underrepresented students because they end up with more debt (i.e., student loans) and will never make up the difference, unless they step outside of the box and develop innovative, profitable ideas. Although STEM fields promise a lucrative career, there are not many underrepresented students who pursue these areas of study.

In his book *Linchpin*, best-selling author Seth Godin encourages his readers to make themselves "indispensable"—unique and innovative, someone who has a set of skills that no one else can duplicate. Students can do this by stepping outside of their comfort zone and taking action toward the career they want.

Once students have decided that they are going to college, it is imperative that they begin to map out the four-year plan, which includes academic, social, and professional goals. Advise students to think holistically, because they will want to develop practical skills along with their college degree that are marketable in multiple fields. Show them how to choose a major that they enjoy and challenges them to think. Not all majors force students to navigate outside of their comfort zone. Taking the easiest professor will not lead you down the road to success.

Students do themselves a disservice when they try to look for a faculty member who only minimally challenges them to do their best. Students will benefit the most from instructors who challenge them. Most instructors want students to succeed. Remember, challenge + rigor + innovation = creativity, which leads to a lifetime of career options.

Students must learn to think ahead; many students are advised to focus solely on their classes during freshman year. However, there are some things that students can do to build their portfolio. From the first time students set foot on campus, they must develop the skills of networking with faculty, administrators, graduate assistants, future employers, and other students. Students will find it surprising that just remembering someone's name or meeting them for coffee every once in a while may cultivate a relationship for a future reference, internship, or job.

Networking does not end there; the student's job is to stay in contact with everyone they meet the rest of their life. So, it's advisable to create a database of contacts with the basic information and include a column at the end that describes how they met the person. This will help you later when you get ready to ask for a recommendation letter, as you will be able to describe when and how you met. Beyond networking for future opportunities, you will need to start thinking about what you will be doing the next summer. Will you intern on campus or somewhere in your field of study?

Learning should not be based in a fad but in building a broad skill set that can be tested and real-world scenarios and experiences—this is intellectual entrepreneurship.

Students cannot properly invest in their future without having a passion for learning. They need experiences and intellectual opportunities to combine areas that they are intensely interested in with areas that they know nothing about.

In choosing a college or major or in maximizing one's intellectual environment, always seek out ways to get a variety of feedback on your ideas beyond the classroom. The college experience of the twenty-first century will provide more opportunities for students to test and creatively apply their ideas than at any point in the past.

THE UN-EXAM: FOUR QUESTIONS YOU MUST ASK OF EVERY CLASS, EVERY DEGREE, EVERY COLLEGE, AND ANYTHING ELSE THAT YOU LEARN

Regardless of what major students choose or whether they choose none at all, they will most certainly face one of these four questions during their lifetime. The decision to commit to learning, whether free or not, should be based on a clear response to these questions:

1. How can I potentially use this information or experiences today, tomorrow, for the rest of my life? What other areas of past learning can I combine with this information to present new questions and new opportunities for myself?
2. Since it is impossible for me to know what the future holds, would committing my time and resources here prevent me from engaging in other pursuits that may be more difficult to monetize today but be potentially more energizing and intellectually relevant to my long-term goals (+10 years)?
3. If time and money were not a factor, would I still be interested in pursuing this? If I had all the time and money I needed, would this be worth learning?
4. How will the acquisition of this knowledge make me a better person?

Knowing the answers to these questions will prepare students for three scenarios that they will certainly face in the near future.

- The student's level of knowledge and skills will not match the level of passion at their job.
- The student's level of knowledge and skills will not match their level of compensation.
- The student will not be able to find any work at all.

Since it is likely that students will face one of these scenarios in their lifetime, it is important to think about college not as a mere credential but as a place to learn a broader set of skills and strategies and a mind-set for survival.

Cultivating a heart for working experience, whether it is through a nonpaid or a paid internship, helps you learn more about yourself. Discovering what you like and don't like to do is an essential part of the process. If you start off as a nursing major and never work in a hospital, then in your junior year you decide it's finally time to jump in and then find out you don't like the work, you've just wasted three years in a major that you will not pursue or use in your lifetime. The earlier start the better off students will be as they navigate their career.

LIFE AFTER COLLEGE

It can get quite stressful when one thinks about what life means after college. But the key is to start your pursuit of employment early, say in your sophomore or junior year. Developing networks with professors, administrators, your current part-time employer, and internship supervisors often leads to opportunities that may not necessarily be posted online. Sixty percent of jobs are received through networking, which has changed the market drastically. Life after college does not have to be hard, as long as you prepare. There are more options for students after college than they could ever imagine, including but not limited to graduate school in another area of study, learning another language, traveling abroad for employment, working in your field of study, or starting your own personal venture (e.g., nonprofit organization or business, etc.).

Scenarios After Graduation

There are several situations that students can expect to encounter when they graduate from college. First, remember that they are not looking for a job. If students followed the steps that we outlined in this book they should already have a job. What students are looking for is an opportunity to expand their skill set and to build on multiple career options that will allow them to pursue their life goals.

If you are aware of a certain employer that other students want to work for, you have already started the process of building a network of contacts at the company, most likely through an internship or even a part-time job. Ideally, students should have a full-time position with an employer lined up before graduation. If they don't have a position, they should be reevaluating their field and whether further education will help. More than likely, their situation will fall into one of the scenarios listed below.

Scenario One

The first situation is that you graduate and are offered a position that pays enough money to cover your living expenses and offers new opportunities for growth and expansion. This is what has been referred to in the past as the American Dream. In the past this meant that students received enough money to buy a home, have at least one car, and enjoy modern conveniences. The generation after World War II expected to work in this same job for thirty years and to retire and receive a good pension to live on. Typically, students will change their career five to seven times in a lifetime. If this is the opportunity that you have been given, take advantage of it and be grateful.

Unfortunately, for most people who are graduating into the workforce this will not be the reality. In today's global marketplace, salaries are very competitive and jobs that offer enough money to afford the amenities listed above are often so specialized that you may not even know that the opportunity for such a career existed—that's why we emphasize thinking about college as a place for discovery, exploration, and experimentation.

Since students compete not only with their classmates at their college or university for these jobs but with people from all over the world who are willing to work for much less than they can afford to, students may find that the salaries that they are being offered today are less than what their parents were being offered when they graduated. More than likely a student's employer will not offer a pension or provide other options for retirement, but one can prepare for this scenario by saving 10 percent of every dollar earned.

Most college graduates will fall into one of the other two scenarios listed below.

Scenario Two

You are offered a position but it is in a field that is not what you went to college to pursue. There is a sad cliché about theater majors waiting tables at restaurants, but the same is true for business, biology, and accounting majors and even people with advanced law degrees. More than likely your position in sales, retail, or perhaps in the restaurant industry is not where you envisioned yourself. Don't be discouraged! The roadmap to your dreams is not always a straight line, sometimes detours are involved. Take advantage of the opportunities to develop skills in these areas but do not let it detract you from your real goal. Keep working and learning about how you can get where you want to be.

Scenario Three

You have found a job in your field of study but it does not offer you the minimum salary that you need because of the lack of experience. However, you have an opportunity to move up the ladder if you stay committed and enroll in a leadership program. You might have to live with your parents or find a roommate to share expenses with for the first year or so. Do you take this opportunity, or choose another route?

Scenario Four

The fourth situation is that you find nothing at all. Hopefully, if you followed the steps outlined in this book, you will not be in this situation because you will have taken advantage of opportunities to create your own career. You may be working in a part-time job on the side, but that's just giving you the money to survive while pursuing what you really want to do.

How to Avoid Scenario Four

When students graduate from college they should already have a job lined up or at least have a revenue stream on the side. Remember, college is not a race. The goal is not to graduate as fast as you can but rather to develop networks, develop core competencies, and expand your knowledge about making a living by using it as a laboratory for inquiry.

It is true that once upon a time college was a ticket to the middle class. Those days simply do not exist anymore. When students graduate they are competing not just with their classmates but with the world. There are people all over the world who have the same skills that they do, and increasingly there are people who have better skills than graduates from some of the best American universities. How can students compete?

While the competition is stiff, there are ways to make students more viable in today's market. Understanding the global economy will take them a long way in their lifetime. It does not matter what they have majored in during their college education. If students can, they should open themselves up to employment internationally. It will provide students not only an income but a diverse living and learning experience that will strengthen their portfolio.

Consider working for organizations such as the Peace Corps or Teach for America. Although the pay may not be as high as you would like, these positions offer the opportunity for you to strengthen your skill set as well as forgiving student loans and providing a benefits package and flexibility. Another option to think about is not necessarily going back to college for another degree but strengthening your development through training programs and learning another language.

CONCLUSION

Ashley understands that college is not something that just happens to students but that they must actively engage it and use it in the ways that they need to accomplish their goals. Her approach to college requires reworking assumptions about the passive investment that many students make at one of the most important junctures of their education. Instead of allowing college to simply happen, Ashley actively hacks college to search for and assemble the experiences that are most meaningful to her. She realizes that there are risks in this process but that her willingness to ask new questions and bring together different fields of knowledge allows her to find opportunities that are unique and that make her more competitive in the international knowledge economy.

What sets Ashley apart from Jason and many of the other typical students outlined here is that she sees college as an investment in herself and not a degree or a fad. The experiences that she seeks out are meaningful not only to her economic goals but to her overall development as a person. She realizes that as college has become more accessible to the masses, the creative aspects of that experience have been curtailed to make it more appealing.

Ashley realizes that while there are some aspects of this mass educational model that she must engage, others are negotiable and can be bartered to create the education that she desires.

ACTION STEPS

1. Show students how to use college education as a tool for lifelong learning instead of a short-term training ground.
2. Refer students to the Bureau of Labor Statistics, O*Net Online, and the *Occupational Outlook Handbook* for ideas and forecast of future economic opportunities. Assist them with viewing these resources as guidance for future opportunities instead of predetermined outcomes.
3. Teach students how to think about accumulated courses as experiences toward learning goals instead of checklist points on a curriculum sheet.
4. Advise students to take numerous skills assessment tests such as the Differential Aptitude Test, Strengths Quest, Myers-Briggs, Discovery, and others. These assessments will give them a better understanding of how their abilities and personalities impact educational aptitude and job performance.
5. Encourage students to find experienced mentors who can help them navigate their college and career goals. This will help them build relationships that will last a lifetime, not just for the duration of a class or a semester.

Conclusion

Students come to college for a variety of reasons—some for the opportunity to gain knowledge and expertise in their field of study, others to attain the status associated with a college degree, but most to increase their earning potential. The primary goal of earning more money means that every student, parent, and advisor must ask certain kinds of questions that have never been the primary focus of higher educational institutions.

The array of concerns posed by students, parents, and stakeholders that we have explored in this book reveal that viewing college exclusively as an investment presents serious problems that can be a major impediment to achieving the intended economic goals. Students are often consigning themselves to a life of poverty far too early and with little forethought. The illusion of a college degree being a guarantee to a life of prosperity has been outrageously marketed by colleges for far too long. These illusions of grandeur have prompted students, parents, and policymakers to miss some of the most valuable lessons that higher education can provide them.

Far too often, students perceive college as a barrier that they must break through, a torture that must be endured, or a distraction from the so-called real world. They undervalue the buffet of knowledge that is open to endless possibilities and answers to the concerns of making a living. Each student profile we have explored in this book reveals how this view hinders student achievement—both academic and economic. The solutions we have proposed in table 7.1, "Profile Student Solutions," are modest but are definitely no panacea.

The reality of the American dream for many middle-class families has become less tangible for a variety of economic, geopolitical, and cultural reasons that are outside the purview of college credentialization.

Table 7.1. Profile Student Solutions

Profile Student	View	Problem	Solution/Action Steps
Jason	College degree will provide a guaranteed income	Not aware of the impact of debt	Seek information about full cost Develop ten-year budget
Heather	College degree will provide guaranteed stability	Not aware of the global competition	Have global experiences Acquire diverse educational skills
Todd	Value in amenities	Overpriced vacation	Satisfy amenities urge elsewhere Explore college budget
Maria	College as solution to inequality	Degree not enough alone	Participate in cultural networks Participate in networks outside of affinity group Find mentor from privileged background
Aimee	College degree is a certificate of deposit	Expects too high return and too soon on wrong commodity	Attend a skills- or trade-oriented institution Invest in entrepreneurship Seek entrepreneurial opportunities
Ashley	College degree is irrelevant and worthless	Fails to see connection between experiences and education	Have global experiences Acquire diverse educational skills Seek entrepreneurial opportunities with mentorship Expand exposure to more diverse content

The core problem with the investment analogy is that many of the assumptions made about college as a sound investment do not appropriately assess the value of the college experience. Value is interpreted solely in linear economic terms and not as a holistic benefit. Furthermore, there are significant assumptions about the marketplace that are based on a presentist perspective that fail to incorporate the possibilities of tomorrow's world. It is often said that colleges are training students today for jobs of tomorrow that do not yet exist.

Critics argue that there are a variety of occupations that are high-paying but that can be attained with an associate degree or less. The problem with this approach is that if we were to revisit this same list in ten years, we would

Conclusion

find that many of the positions on that list will be obsolete or the demand will have evaporated. When we base a college experience on such a narrow technical mandate we plan for obsolescence.

More disturbing, when we force students to make such narrow-minded decisions about college and career planning based on salary projections alone, we assume that they are less equipped to be the innovators of the future. We relegate them, intellectually and academically, to a circumscribed second-class education.

On the other hand, if students, parents, policymakers, and other stakeholders look at college education as providing a broad foundation for a certain skill set that empowers students to think critically, creatively, and laterally, we "invest" in a future that makes it possible for graduates to retrain and retool themselves as the economy shifts. While it is certainly essential for students seeking a college education to think about market forces, students must not lose sight of the broader value of college.

Perhaps it is more useful to think of college in the same way that individuals think of churches, mosques, and synagogues. These institutions are important not so much for the credentials that they bestow or services rendered at the point of delivery, but much more so for the values that they promote. We could ask, and many have, if it is harmful to society to divest such a large amount of taxpayer money to promote religious values that have no correlation to productivity or profitability.

If you were to ask parishioners whether they thought they were getting their money's worth, more than likely they would be taken aback by such an inquiry. However, if parishioners felt that their needs were not adequately being addressed in their house of worship or that their clergy were wasting the resources that had been bestowed to them, we know that many people would simply vote with their feet to an institution that better met their spiritual and emotional needs.

Colleges are not houses of worship but they are sacred spaces in our democracy. Ultimately, student success during and following the college years depends on so much more than a good investment strategy based on salary expectations alone. Students need a sustained commitment from parents, educators, administrators, and policymakers to provide for their complex needs, but the current design of the college experience means they must initiate and demand these opportunities.

The outcome of a college education includes not only the student's efforts but the institution's commitment to addressing the broader socioeconomic context preceding and following the college years. Attempting to isolate cost as a factor without interrogating its broader goals, mission, impact, and possibilities distorts the meaning of the college experience for students and its ultimate economic worth.

Because our discussion of college has been so rooted in the norms and elusive goals of outdated concepts of the value and goals of learning, we have failed to incorporate a true understanding of how privilege and the challenges of a globalizing economy have shaped notions of opportunity, progress, and true education for most students today.

This dilemma brings to mind the image of the child attempting to snatch the floating dollar. The boy is oblivious to the man dangling the dollar from the fishing pole with an invisible line. As long as the child focuses solely on the dollar, he cannot see the thread connected to the fishing rod. Once the boy realizes that he is the brunt of the old man's joke, the dollar is his for the taking. We find this an appropriate analogy for the current pursuit of college as an investment. As long as students focus solely on the economic value of college as a credential, more often than not it becomes an elusive and frustrating goal.

For many students, college has been a cruel joke denying them the economic prosperity that attracted them to pursue a degree in the first place. For other students, they realize a deeper lesson. College was not meant to deceive or defraud them. It was never designed to do that in the first place. Rather, college is a learning experience, an insightful moment that provides a broad experiment in human interaction and understanding. As these lessons are gleaned, the material pursuits become less meaningful but more attainable and the investment seems less lousy.

Bibliography

"Adaptability to Online Learning: Differences Across Types of Students and Academic Subject Areas." Accessed March 26, 2014. http://ccrc.tc.columbia.edu/media/k2/attachments/adaptability-to-online-learning.pdf.

Adler, Lou. "New Survey Reveals 85% of All Jobs Are Filled Via Networking." LinkedIn Pulse, February 29, 2016. https://www.linkedin.com/pulse/new-survey-reveals-85-all-jobs-filled-via-networking-lou-adler.

Alon, Sigal. "Who Benefits Most from Financial Aid? The Heterogeneous Effect of Need-Based Grants on Students' College Persistence." *Social Science Quarterly* 92, no. 3 (September 1, 2011): 807–29. doi:10.1111/j.1540-6237.2011.00793.x.

Alva, Jorge Klor de, Mark Schneider, and American Institutes for Research. "Who Wins? Who Pays? The Economic Returns and Costs of a Bachelor's Degree." American Institutes for Research, May 1, 2011.

Anders, George. "Good News Liberal-Arts Majors: Your Peers Probably Won't Outearn You Forever." *Wall Street Journal*, September 12, 2016, sec. Markets. http://www.wsj.com/articles/good-news-liberal-arts-majors-your-peers-probably-wont-outearn-you-forever-1473645902.

Arum, Richard, and Josipa Roksa. *Academically Adrift: Limited Learning on College Campuses.* Chicago: University of Chicago Press, 2011.

Bauerlein, Mark. *The Dumbest Generation: How the Digital Age Stupefies Young Americans and Jeopardizes Our Future (or, Don't Trust Anyone under 30).* New York: Jeremy P. Tarcher/Penguin, 2008.

Baum, Sandy, and Patricia Steele. "Who Borrows Most? Bachelor's Degree Recipients with High Levels of Student Debt." Trends in Higher Education, The College Board, April 2010. https://trends.collegeboard.org/content/who-borrows-most-bachelors-degree-recipients-high-levels-student-debt-april-2010.

Bennett, Michael, and Jacqueline Brady. "A Radical Critique of the Learning Outcomes Assessment Movement," *The Radical Teacher*, no. 94 (Fall 2012): 34–47.

Bennett, William J., and David Wilezol. *Is College Worth It: A Former United States Secretary of Education and a Liberal Arts Graduate Expose the Broken Promise of Higher Education.* Nashville, TN: Thomas Nelson, 2013.

Bertrand, Marianne, and Sendhil Mullainathan. "Are Emily and Greg More Employable Than Lakisha and Jamal? A Field Experiment on Labor Market Discrimination." Working Paper. National Bureau of Economic Research, July 2003. http://www.nber.org/papers/w9873.

Borrup, Tom, and Borrup, Thomas C. *Creative Community Builder's Handbook: How to Transform Communities Using Local Assets, Arts, and Culture.* Saint Paul, MN : Fieldstone Alliance, 2006.

Bourdabat, B. and Montmarquette, C. "Choice Fields of Study of University Canadian Graduates: The Role of Gender and their Parents' Education." *Education Economics*, 17(2) (June 1, 2009): 185–213.

Bowman, Nicholas A., Julie J. Park, and Nida Denson. (2014) "Student Involvement in Ethnic Student Organizations: Examining Civic Outcomes 6 Years After Graduation," *Research in Higher Education*, vol. 56, no. 2 (March 2015): 127–45.

Bowen, William G., Derek Bok, Glenn C. Loury, et al. *The Shape of the River*. Princeton, NJ: Princeton University Press, 2000.

Bozick, Robert, Eric Lauff, John Wirt, and Washington Institute of Education Sciences. "Education Longitudinal Study of 2002 (ELS:2002): A First Look at the Initial Postsecondary Experiences of the High School Sophomore Class of 2002." National Center for Education Statistics, October 1, 2007.

Carlson, Scott. "How to Assess the Real Payoff of a College Degree." *Chronicle of Higher Education* 59, no. 33 (April 26, 2013): A26–32.

Charette, Robert N. (2013). "Is It Fair to Steer Students into STEM Disciplines Facing a Glut of Workers?" *IEEE Spectrum*. https://spectrum.ieee.org/riskfactor/at-work/tech-careers/stem-crisis-as-myth-gets-yet-another-workout.

Che, Jenny. "Wages for College Grads Are Now Lower Than They Were 15 Years Ago." *Huffington Post*, June 2, 2015, http://www.huffingtonpost.com/2015/06/02/low-college-grads-salary_n_7484204.html.

Cipriano, Bob, and Richard, Riccardi L. "The Changes One Department Made to Increase Student Engagement and Graduation Rates." *Recruitment & Retention in Higher Education* 22, no. 1 (January 2008): 4–5.

Clifford, Catherine. "These 20 Kids Just Got $100,000 to Drop Out of School. And They Want to Change Your Life." *Entrepreneur*, June 5, 2014. https://www.entrepreneur.com/article/234544.

Clynes, Tom. "Peter Thiel's Dropout Army." *The New York Times*, June 4, 2016. http://www.nytimes.com/2016/06/05/opinion/sunday/peter-thiels-dropout-army.html.

"College Education Value Rankings— PayScale 2013 College ROI Report." *PayScale* . Accessed April 24, 2014. http://www.payscale.com/college-education-value.

"College, Inc. | FRONTLINE | PBS." Accessed December 25, 2016. http://www.pbs.org/wgbh/pages/frontline/collegeinc/.

Cotter, David A., Joan M. Hermsen, Seth Ovadia, and Reeve Vanneman. "The Glass Ceiling Effect." *Social Forces* 80, no. 2 (December 1, 2001): 655–81.

CQ Press Staff. "Report on U.S. College Curriculum—February 11, 1985." In *Historic Documents of 1985*, 14th ed., Annual, revised. Vol. 14. Washington, DC: CQ Press, 1986. http://knowledge.sagepub.com/view/historic-documents-of-1985/SAGE.xml.

Dancy, Kim. "Who Takes Out Parent PLUS Loans Anyway." New America, January 13, 2016, accessed January 1, 2017, https://www.newamerica.org/education-policy/edcentral/parent-plus-loans/.

Davis, Dannielle Joy. "Access to Academe: The Importance of Mentoring to Black Students." *Negro Educational Review* 58 (2007).

Desmond-Harris, Jenée. "If I Were a Poor Black Kid Responses." *The Root*, Dec. 16, 2011. http://www.theroot.com/articles/culture/2011/12/if_i_were_a_poor_black_kid_responses.html.

Elliott, William, and IlSung Nam. "Is Student Debt Jeopardizing the Short-Term Financial Health of U.S. Households?" *Federal Reserve Bank of St. Louis Review* , October 9, 2013.

Fiegerman, Seth. "Bill Gates: Don't Call Me a College Dropout." *Mashable*. Accessed November 3, 2016. http://mashable.com/2014/02/10/bill-gates-ama-2/.

"Fighting to Free Knowledge Paid for by Taxpayers—And Winning." *Techdirt* . Accessed April 23, 2014. http://www.techdirt.com/articles/20131001/09404524712/fighting-to-free-knowledge-paid-taxpayers-winning.shtml.

Florida, Richard. "The Rise of the Creative Class, Revisited." Accessed December 21, 2016. http://www.creativeclass.com/rfcgdb/articles/national%20journal%20Rise%20of%20the%20Creative%20Class.pdf.

———. *The Rise of the Creative Class, Revisited: 10th Anniversary Edition—Revised and Expanded*. 2nd edition. New York: Basic Books, 2012.
Fossey, Richard. *Condemning Students to Debt: College Loans and Public Policy*. Williston, VT: Teachers College Press, 1998. https://eric.ed.gov/?id=ED430434.
Freire, Paulo. *Pedagogy of the Oppressed*. New York: Continuum, 2003.
Fry, Richard. "A Record One-in-Five Households Now Owe Student Loan Debt." *Pew Research Center's Social & Demographic Trends Project*, September 26, 2012. http://www.pewsocialtrends.org/2012/09/26/a-record-one-in-five-households-now-owe-student-loan-debt/.
Fry, Richard. "The Changing Profile of Student Borrowers," PewResearchCenter, October 7, 2014, accessed January 1, 2017, http://www.pewsocialtrends.org/2014/10/07/the-changing-profile-of-student-borrowers/.
Gates, Bill. "Help Wanted: 11 Million College Grads." Accessed November 3, 2016. https://www.gatesnotes.com/Education/11-Million-College-Grads.
Ginsberg, Benjamin. *The Fall of the Faculty*. Reprint edition. New York: Oxford University Press, 2013.
Godin, Seth. *Linchpin: Are You Indispensable?* New York: Penguin Group, 2010.
Goldrick-Rab, Sara, Douglas N. Harris, and Philip A. Trostel . "Why Financial Aid Matters (or Does Not) for College Success: Toward a New Interdisciplinary Perspective." In *Higher Education: Handbook of Theory and Research*, edited by John C. Smart, 1–45. Netherlands: Springer, 2009. http://link.springer.com/chapter/10.1007/978-1-4020-9628-0_1.
"Grading Student Loans Liberty Street Economics." Accessed November 3, 2016. http://libertystreeteconomics.newyorkfed.org/2012/03/grading-student-loans.html.
Griffin, Kimberly, Wilfredo del Pilar, Kadian McIntosh, and Autumn Griffin. "'Oh, of Course I'm Going to Go to College': Understanding How Habitus Shapes the College Choice Process of Black Immigrant Students." *Journal of Diversity in Higher Education* 5, no. 2 (June 2012): 96–111. doi:10.1037/a0028393.
Grove, Cornelius. *The Drive to Learn: What the East Asian Experience Tells Us About Raising Students Who Excel*. Lanham, MD: Rowman and Littlefield, 2017.
Hayes, Dianne. "The For-Profit Conundrum." *Diverse: Issues in Higher Education* 29, no. 14 (August 16, 2012): 10–11.
Henderson, Cathy, American Council on Education, and Division of Policy Analysis and Research. *College Debts of Recent Graduates* . Washington, DC: American Council on Education, Division of Policy Analysis and Research, 1987. http://files.eric.ed.gov/fulltext/ED288474.pdf.
Hersh, Richard H. "Intention and Perceptions A National Survey of Public Attitudes Toward Liberal Arts Education." *Change: The Magazine of Higher Learning* 29, no. 2 (March 1, 1997): 16–23. doi:10.1080/00091389709603100.
"Higher Education Research Institute." Accessed November 7, 2016. http://heri.ucla.edu/prdisplay.php?prQry=111.
"Higher Education: What's the Social Benefit of College?" *AnnArbor.com*. Accessed April 23, 2014. http://www.annarbor.com/passions-pursuits/higher-education-whats-the-social-value-of-college/.
"Home." *The Thiel Fellowship*. Accessed December 21, 2016. http://thielfellowship.org/.
hooks, bell. *Teaching to Transgress: Education as the Practice of Freedom*. New York: Routledge, 1994.
Hout, Michael. "Social and Economic Returns to College Education in the United States." *Annual Review of Sociology* 38, no. 1 (2012): 379–400. doi:10.1146/annurev.soc.012809.102503.
"How Do Young People Choose College Majors?" Accessed September 18, 2016. http://citeseerx.ist.psu.edu/viewdoc/download?doi=10.1.1.606.4138&rep=rep1&type=pdf.
Huelsman, Mark. *The Debt Divide: The Racial and Class Bias Behind the "New Normal" of Student Borrowing*. New York: Demos, 2018.
"Hunting for Soft Skills, Companies Scoop Up English Majors." Accessed October 31, 2016. http://finance.yahoo.com/news/hunting-soft-skills-companies-scoop-140100691.html.

"If I Were A Poor Black Kid." *Forbes.* Accessed April 7, 2014. http://www.forbes.com/sites/quickerbettertech/2011/12/12/if-i-was-a-poor-black-kid/.

"If the 'New Challenges' Link Doesn't Work, Use This! Learning Communities Faculty Scholars." Accessed July 5, 2016. https://kennesaw.view.usg.edu/d2l/le/content/761573/full-screen/14229850/View.

Ikard, David. *Breaking the Silence: Toward a Black Male Feminist Criticism.* LSU Press, 2007.

"I'm Glad I Dropped Out of College by Steve Jobs." Accessed November 3, 2016, http://archive.lewrockwell.com/rep2/steve-jobs-speech-2005.html.

"Is College Worth It?" *The Economist,* April 5, 2014, http://www.economist.com/news/united-states/21600131-too-many-degrees-are-waste-money-return-higher-education-would-be-much-better.

"Is College Worth It? College Presidents, Public Assess Value, Quality and Mission of Higher Education." Accessed December 24, 2016, http://www.pewsocialtrends.org/files/2011/05/higher-ed-report.pdf.

"Is College Worth It?" Pew Research Center, May 15, 2011, accessed January 1, 2017, http://www.pewsocialtrends.org/2011/05/15/is-college-worth-it/.

"Is College Worth It? Goldman Sachs says maybe not." CNN Money, December 9, 2015, accessed January 1, 2017, http://money.cnn.com/2015/12/09/news/economy/college-not-worth-it-goldman/

"It Takes Half as Long to Recoup the Cost of a College Degree Today as It Did in the 1970s." *Washington Post,* accessed October 31, 2016, https://www.washingtonpost.com/news/get-there/wp/2014/09/03/it-takes-half-as-long-to-recoup-the-cost-of-a-college-degree-today-as-it-did-in-the-1970s/.

Jacob, Brian, Brian McCall, and Kevin M. Stange. "College as Country Club: Do Colleges Cater to Students' Preferences for Consumption?" Working Paper. National Bureau of Economic Research, January 2013. http://www.nber.org/papers/w18745.

Jobs, Steve. "Staying Hungry." *Reed Magazine | Sallyportal,* Accessed November 3, 2016, http://www.reed.edu/reed_magazine/sallyportal/posts/2013/staying-hungry.html.

Kasal Fusco, Linda. *Navigating Mathland: How Parents Can Help Their Kids through the Maze.* Lanham, MD: Rowman and Littlefield, 2017.

Ke, Fengfeng, and Dean Kwak. "Online Learning across Ethnicity and Age: A Study on Learning Interaction Participation, Perception, and Learning Satisfaction." *Computers & Education* 61 (February 2013): 43–51. doi:10.1016/j.compedu.2012.09.003.

Kelchen, Robert. "An Analysis of Student Fees: The Roles of States and Institutions." *The Review of Higher Education* 39, no. 4 (June 13, 2016): 597–619. doi:10.1353/rhe.2016.0027.

Keup, Jennifer R. "New Challenges in Working with Traditional-Aged College Students." *New Directions for Higher Education,* no. 144 (January 1, 2008): 27–37.

Labaree, David F. *How to Succeed in School Without Really Learning: The Credentials Race in American Education.* New Haven, CT: Yale University Press, 1997.

Lacy, Sarah. "Peter Thiel: We're in a Bubble and It's Not the Internet. It's Higher Education." *TechCrunch,* accessed December 25, 2016, http://social.techcrunch.com/2011/04/10/peter-thiel-were-in-a-bubble-and-its-not-the-internet-its-higher-education/.

"LendEDU's Student Loan Debt Statistics by State by School Report." *Lendedu,* accessed January 19, 2017, https://lendedu.com/blog/student-loan-debt-statistics-by-state-by-school.

Lemons, Gary L. *Black Male Outsider: Teaching as a Pro-Feminist Man.* New York: SUNY Press, 2008.

Lobosco, Katie. "Students Are Graduating with $30,000 in loans." CNN Money, October 18, 2016, accessed January 1, 2017, http://money.cnn.com/2016/10/18/pf/college/average-student-loan-debt/.

Marchand, Ashley. "Black Graduates Owe More Debt Than White, Asian, or Hispanic Graduates." *The Chronicle of Higher Education,* April 26, 2010. http://chronicle.com/article/Black-Graduates-Owe-More-Debt/65253/.

"Mark Zuckerberg." Accessed November 3, 2016. http://editoria.let.uniroma1.it/multimediale/files/Time_Zuckerberg.pdf.

Naish, John. "The Web Is a Human Meta-Brain." *New Statesman* 140, no. 5066 (August 15, 2011): 32–35.

Newfield, Christopher. *Unmaking the Public University: The Forty-Year Assault on the Middle Class*. Reprint edition. Cambridge, MA: Harvard University Press, 2011.

Newlon, Cara. "The College Amenities Arms Race." *Forbes*, July 31, 2014, accessed January 2, 2017, http://www.forbes.com/sites/caranewlon/2014/07/31/the-college-amenities-arms-race/#21c0e4671f3c.

"Nicolescu_f.pdf." Accessed April 23, 2014. http://www.learndev.org/dl/nicolescu_f.pdf.

Ossola, Alexandra. "Is the U.S. Focusing Too Much on STEM?" *The Atlantic*, December 3, 2014, http://www.theatlantic.com/education/archive/2014/12/is-the-us-focusing-too-much-on-stem/383353/.

Parker, Wendy. "The Story of Grutter v. Bollinger." Accessed May 30, 2014. http://users.wfu.edu/mcclanas/bookchapter.pdf.

Paulsen, Michael B., and Edward P. St. John. "Social Class and College Costs: Examining the Financial Nexus Between College Choice and Persistence." *The Journal of Higher Education* 73, no. 2 (2002): 189–236. doi:10.1353/jhe.2002.0023.

Perna, Laura Walter. "Differences in the Decision to Attend College among Blacks, Hispanics, and Whites." *The Journal of Higher Education* 71, No. 2 (March–April 2000): 117–141.

"Peter Thiel: We're in a Bubble and It's Not the Internet. It's Higher Education." Accessed Nov. 3, 2016. http://www.immagic.com/eLibrary/ARCHIVES/GENERAL/GENPRESS/T110410L.pdf.

Pew Research Center. "Is College Worth It?" *Pew Research Center's Social & Demographic Trends Project*, May 15, 2011, http://www.pewsocialtrends.org/files/2011/05/higher-ed-report.pdf.

Pollan, Stephen. *Die Broke: A Radical Four-Part Financial Plan*. New York: HarperBusiness, 1997.

Powell, Walter, and Kaisa Snellman. "The Knowledge Economy." Accessed November 13, 2016, http://scholar.harvard.edu/files/kaisa/files/powell_snellman.pdf.

Price, Derek V. *Borrowing Inequality: Race, Class, and Student Loans*. Boulder, CO: L. Rienner Publishers, 2004.

"Reed College | Steve Jobs and Reed." Accessed November 3, 2016, http://www.reed.edu/steve-jobs.

Reilly, Peter J. "When Will the Education Bubble Explode?" *Forbes*. Accessed December 25, 2016. http://www.forbes.com/sites/peterjreilly/2011/11/02/when-will-the-education-bubble-explode/.

Richardson, John T. E. "Face-to-Face versus Online Tuition: Preference, Performance and Pass Rates in White and Ethnic Minority Students." *British Journal of Educational Technology* 43, no. 1 (January 1, 2012): 17–27.

Robinson, Eugene. *Disintegration: The Splintering of Black America*. Reprint. New York: Anchor, 2011.

Samuelson, Robert J. "It's Time to Drop the College-for-All Crusade." *The Washington Post*, May 27, 2012. https://www.washingtonpost.com/opinions/its-time-to-drop-the-college-for-all-crusade/2012/05/27/gJQAzcUGvU_story.html.

"Saying No to College." Accessed November 3, 2016. http://www.alamo.edu/uploadedFiles/District/About_Us/Chancellor/family_memo_pdfs/Saying-No-to-College-NYTimes.pdf.

Schoen, John W. "The Real Reasons a College Degree Costs So Much." *CNBC*, June 16, 2015. http://www.cnbc.com/2015/06/16/why-college-costs-are-so-high-and-rising.html.

Selingo, Jeffrey J. *College (Un)bound: The Future of Higher Education and What It Means for Students*. Boston: Houghton Mifflin Harcourt, 2013.

Selingo, Jeffrey J. *There Is Life After College: What Parents and Students Should Know About Navigating School to Prepare for the Jobs of Tomorrow*. New York: William Morrow, 2016.

Shapiro, Thomas M. *The Hidden Cost of Being African American: How Wealth Perpetuates Inequality*. New York: Oxford University Press, 2004.

Simkovic, Michael. "Risk-Based Student Loans." SSRN Scholarly Paper. Rochester, New York: *Social Science Research Network*, September 5, 2011. https://papers.ssrn.com/abstract=1941070.

Simmons, Charlene Wear. "Student Loans for Higher Education." Accessed November 5, 2016. http://www.library.ca.gov/crb/08/08-002.pdf.

Staff, Ashly Perez BuzzFeed Motion Pictures. "23 Famous Dropouts Who Turned Out Just Fine." *BuzzFeed*, accessed October 31, 2016. http://www.buzzfeed.com/ashleyperez/23-famous-dropouts-who-turned-out-just-fine.

Steele, Claude M. "Thin Ice: Stereotype Threat and Black College Students." *The Atlantic*, August 1999. http://www.theatlantic.com/magazine/archive/1999/08/thin-ice-stereotype-threat-and-black-college-students/304663/.

"Steve Jobs—Commencement Address at Stanford University (2005)." *Genius*, accessed November 3, 2016. http://genius.com/Steve-jobs-commencement-address-at-stanford-university-2005-annotated.

"Steve Jobs: Stanford Commencement Address, June 2005." Accessed November 3, 2016, http://clarksite.com/wp-content/uploads/2011/10/Stanford-commencement-address-June-2005-Technology-The-Observer.pdf.

"Steven P. Jobs '76." *Reed Magazine | In Memoriam*. Accessed November 3, 2016, http://www.reed.edu/reed_magazine/in-memoriam/obituaries/december2011/steve-jobs-1976.html.

"Student Loan Debt Statistics for 2017." *Lendedu*, July 1, 2016, https://lendedu.com/blog/student-loan-debt-statistics.

"Students Taking Easy Subject Options Says SCEGGS Darlinghurst Principal Jenny Allum ." *The Sydney Morning Herald*. Accessed April 23, 2014, http://www.smh.com.au/national/education/students-taking-easy-subject-options-says-sceggs-darlinghurst-principal-jenny-allum-20131210-2z42c.html.

"Summary of Sen. Sanders' College for All Act." Accessed November 13, 2016, https://www.sanders.senate.gov/download/collegeforallsummary/?inline=file.

Taubman, Paul J., and Terence Wales. "Higher Education and Earnings: College as an Investment and Screening Device." NBER Books. National Bureau of Economic Research, Inc., 1974. https://ideas.repec.org/b/nbr/nberbk/taub74-1.html.

Taubman, Paul J., and Terrence Wells. "Higher Education and Earnings: College as an Investment and Screening Device." Accessed November 5, 2016, http://www.nber.org/chapters/c3646.pdf.

"The College Bubble (incl. Education & Student Loan Bubble)." Accessed December 25, 2016. http://www.thebubblebubble.com/college-bubble/.

"The Debt Divide: The Racial and Class Bias Behind the 'New Normal' of Student Borrowing | Demos." Accessed December 24, 2016, http://www.demos.org/publication/debt-divide-racial-and-class-bias-behind-new-normal-student-borrowing.

Tierney, Mike. "At Spelman, Dropping Sports in Favor of Fitness." *The New York Times*, April 13, 2013, sec. Sports. http://www.nytimes.com/2013/04/14/sports/at-spelman-dropping-sports-in-favor-of-fitness.html.

"Trends in College Spending: 1998–2008." Accessed November 7, 2016, http://www.deltacostproject.org/sites/default/files/products/Trends-in-College-Spending-98-08.pdf.

"Tuition at Public Colleges Has Soared in the Past Decade, but Student Fees Have Risen Faster." *Washington Post*, accessed January 24, 2017, https://www.washingtonpost.com/news/grade-point/wp/2016/06/22/tuition-at-public-colleges-has-soared-in-the-last-decade-but-student-fees-have-risen-faster/.

Twale, Darla Jean, and Barbara M. De Luca. *Faculty Incivility: The Rise of the Academic Bully Culture and What to Do about It*. Hoboken, NJ: Jossey-Bass, 2008.

Tyler, Lucia D., and Henninger, Susan E. *The Ultimate Guide to College Transfer: From Surviving to Thriving*. Lanham, MD: Rowman and Littlefield, 2017.

Vaught, Seneca, and Jabbaar-Gyambrah, Tara. "Why College as an Investment Is a Lousy Analogy." *Journal of College Admission* No. 226 (Winter 2015), 24–29.

Vital, Anna. "Famous Entrepreneurs Who Dropped Out of College." *Funders and Founders*, March 25, 2014, http://fundersandfounders.com/entrepreneurs-who-dropped-out/.

"What Can I Do with an Economics Degree? | Prospects.ac. uk ." Accessed December 22, 2016, https://www.prospects.ac.uk/careers-advice/what-can-i-do-with-my-degree/economics.

"Why Black Studies Matters." *Discover Society* . Accessed July 6, 2015, http://discoversociety.org/2013/11/05/why-black-studies-matters/.

"Why the Education Bubble Will Be Worse Than the Housing Bubble." *US News & World Report*. Accessed December 25, 2016, http://www.usnews.com/opinion/blogs/economic-intelligence/2012/06/12/the-government-shouldnt-subsidize-higher-education.

Wolf, Alison. *Does Education Matter?: Myths About Education and Economic Growth*. London: Penguin UK, 2002.

Woody, Bette, Diane Brown, and TeResa Green. "Black Women in the Economy: Facing Glass Ceilings in Academia." *Trotter Review* 12, no. 1 (January 1, 2000). http://scholarworks.umb.edu/trotter_review/vol12/iss1/8.

Xu, Di, and Shanna Smith Jaggars. "Adaptability to Online Learning: Differences Across Types of Students and Academic Subject Areas." Community College Research Center Teachers College, Columbia University, February 2013. http://ccrc.tc.columbia.edu/media/k2/attachments/adaptability-to-online-learning.pdf.

Xue, Yi, and Richard Larson. "STEM Crisis or STEM Surplus? Yes and Yes," Monthly Labor Review, U.S. Bureau of Labor Statistics, May 2015, https://doi.org/10.21916/mlr.2015.14.

Zara, Ernest III. *Helping Parents to Understand the Minds and Hearts of Generation Z*. Lanham, MD: Rowman and Littlefield, 2017.

Zhan, Min. "Debt and College Graduation: Differences by Race/Ethnicity." CSD Working Papers, No.13-08, 2013. http://csd.wustl.edu/Publications/Documents/WP13-08.pdf.

Zwilling, Martin. "Drop Out Like Zuckerberg? No. Learn to Be an Entrepreneur in School." *Entrepreneur*, November 7, 2014. https://www.entrepreneur.com/article/239316.

About the Authors

Tara Jabbaar-Gyambrah is an education director of workforce development in Buffalo, New York; an advocate for student success; and a recipient of the John B. Muir award for an author who makes the most significant contribution to the NACAC's *Journal of College Admissions*. She is also an adjunct professor in the Sociology Department at Niagara University. Her life's mission is to empower and equip individuals to reach their maximum potential in their lives.

Seneca Vaught is an associate professor of History and Interdisciplinary Studies at Kennesaw State University who combines his expertise in policy and applied historical methods to address contemporary problems.

www.ingramcontent.com/pod-product-compliance
Lightning Source LLC
Chambersburg PA
CBHW021800230426
43669CB00006B/152